ADHD and the Criminal Justice System

ADHD and the Criminal Justice System

By

Robert Francis Eme

Cambridge Scholars Publishing

ADHD and the Criminal Justice System

By Robert Francis Eme

This book first published 2018

Cambridge Scholars Publishing

Lady Stephenson Library, Newcastle upon Tyne, NE6 2PA, UK

British Library Cataloguing in Publication Data
A catalogue record for this book is available from the British Library

ISBN (10): 1-5275-1335-1
ISBN (13): 978-1-5275-1335-8

TABLE OF CONTENTS

INTRODUCTION

Despite the continuing controversies surrounding Attention-Deficit/Hyperactivity Disorder (ADHD) and periodic media flare-ups which portray ADHD with derision, ridicule, and stigmatization (Barkley, 2017; Hinshaw, 2018; Hinshaw & Ellison, 2016), voluminous research has incontrovertibly established that ADHD is a valid disorder, i.e., a constellation of symptoms caused by impairments in a set of psychological abilities that results in an increased risk for adverse outcomes in multiple areas of life (Barkley, 2015a; Faraone et al., 2015; Nigg, 2016, 2017a; Thapar & Cooper, 2016). This explains why all major medical and psychological associations and government health agencies recognize ADHD as a valid disorder. These agencies include: *American Academy of Child and Adolescent Psychiatry, American Academy of Pediatrics, American Medical Association, American Psychiatric Association, American Psychological Association,* and *U.S. Surgeon General.* One of the adverse outcomes is increased risk for criminal behavior. An astounding 25% of young male adults who are incarcerated in the United States (U.S.), the United Kingdom, and other Western countries have ADHD (Eme & Young, 2017; Young et al., 2015). This represents an approximate three to fourfold greater prevalence of ADHD than exists in the general young adult population (Kessler et al., 2006; Thomas et al., 2015). However, as Dr. Susan Young, one of the foremost authorities in the assessment and treatment of individuals with ADHD in the criminal justice system noted, "in all the research I have conducted in this field, very few have ever been diagnosed with ADHD" (Young, 2017).[1] In addition, many prisoners with ADHD are misdiagnosed because they are presenting to prison healthcare for mood problems or distress that is not recognized as ADHD (Young, 2014). This neglect is all the more egregious given that treatment of individuals with ADHD with stimulant medication can result in a 31% reduction in their criminal behavior (Lichtenstein et al., 2012) and a 43% reduction in violent crime in offenders after release from prison (Chang, Lichtenstein, Langstrom, Larrson, & Fazel, 2016a). Hence, the identification and appropriate

[1] Dr. Young is a clinical senior lecturer in forensic clinical psychology in the Centre for Mental Health, Imperial College London.

management of individuals with ADHD in the criminal justice system is a very promising intervention for reducing the staggering recidivism rate such that within three years of release about two-thirds of offenders are rearrested (Durose, Cooper, & Snyder, 2014).

A tremendous amount of research has been published on ADHD with more than 10,000 studies dating from medical descriptions in 1775 (Barkley, 2015a). An additional 800-1000 studies are added annually, making ADHD the most widely studied disorder affecting children (Barkley, 2015a; Nigg, 2017a). Despite this voluminous literature, this is the first current book written for professionals in the criminal justice system to help them better understand and work with people who have ADHD. It will provide criminal justice professionals with what they need to know about ADHD based on the best of current science. Findings that are especially relevant to understanding how ADHD increases risk for criminal behavior will be highlighted. These findings will be illustrated by vignettes of individuals with ADHD, including those involved in the criminal justice system, in order to provide the reader a deeper understanding of the disorder.[2]

Lastly, the book will focus on males for two reasons. First, until very recently, almost all research on ADHD was conducted exclusively with male samples (Hinshaw, 2018; Owens, Cardoos, & Hinshaw, 2015). Second, as with ADHD, most research on crime is conducted on males since "The fundamental correlate of crime is sex" (DeLisi & Vaughn, p.20) as "Women are always and everywhere less likely than men to commit criminal acts" (Fox, 2017, p.1). For instance, in the U.S., males account for 89.3% of all prisoners and 90% of the homicides (DuRose et al., 2014; Fox, 2017). This sex difference is even more extreme for serious lifelong forms of criminal behavior in which the male-female ratio is in the range of 15-20:1 (DeLisi & Vaugh, 2016). Thus, given this massive sex difference in criminal behavior, it is almost inevitable that research conducted on any risk factor for criminal behavior will be conducted primarily on males.

[2] Many of the examples of those in the criminal justice system are based upon the experiences of Patrick Hurley who is an adult with ADHD with extensive experience in law enforcement and corrections work. He worked as a law enforcement officer for 17 years and as an adult probation/parole officer for 5 years. These experiences provided him with an invaluable perspective on how ADHD can present in a criminal justice setting.

CHAPTER ONE

NATURE OF ADHD

Mental health disorders are defined as a constellation of symptoms and symptom related-distress to the person and/or impairment in one or more important domains of functioning (American Psychiatric Association [APA], 2013). ADHD is the diagnosis given to individuals in the Diagnostic and Statistical Manual of Mental Disorders-5 [DSM-5] (APA, 2013) who present with extreme, impairing symptoms of inattention, impulsivity, and hyperactivity. The diagnosis of ADHD in the DSM-5 is broadly equivalent to the diagnosis of "hyperkinetic disorder" in the World Health Organization's international classification of Diseases 10th edition that is predominantly used in Europe (Thapar & Cooper, 2016). The symptoms producing impairment must occur across more than one setting (e.g., home and school) and must onset by age 12. Although ADHD is typically conceptualized as a disorder of childhood, it is now clear from numerous studies that have followed-up individuals diagnosed with childhood ADHD into late adolescence and young adulthood (as will subsequently be discussed) that the majority of such individuals continue to have impairing symptoms (Asherson, Butelaar, Faraone, & Rohde, 2016; Barkley, 2016a; Hechtman, 2017; Hinshaw, 2018; Thapar & Cooper, 2016). This finding is of special importance for those working in the criminal justice system as many may still believe, as was not uncommon in the recent past, that ADHD is exclusively a disorder of childhood that is outgrown (Hechtman, 2017). In the DSM-5, ADHD is placed in the category of neurodevelopmental disorders. The term *neurodevelopmental* refers to a broad group of disabilities involving some form of disruption of brain development as seen in disorders such as Autism Spectrum Disorder and Intellectual Disability (Thapar, Cooper, & Rutter, 2017). The placement in this category represents a change from previous versions of the DSM in which ADHD was placed in the disruptive behaviors section (Beauchaine & Klein, 2017). The reason for the change was based on (a) evidence for abnormal brain functioning paralleling the aberrant brain functioning in the other neurodevelopmental disorders, and (b) hope that classifying ADHD as a neurodevelopmental disorder would lead to an early diagnosis (Beauchaine & Klein, 2017). Unfortunately, especially for the purposes of this book, this change obscures the causal connections of ADHD to the subsequent development of increasingly severe antisocial behaviors across development (Beauchaine, Zisner, & Sauder, 2017a).

Another alteration from the previous DSM-IV version was to change *subtypes* to presentations because of the recognition that although the diagnosis of ADHD itself is quite stable over time, the assigned presentation is relatively unstable, fluctuating over development (Beauchaine & Klein, 2017; Rooney & Pfiffner, 2018). The three main "presentations" of ADHD in the DSM-5 are: predominantly hyperactive-impulsive, predominantly inattentive (most common presentation of ADHD in community settings, Willcutt, 2012), and the combined form when criteria are met for both inattentive and hyperactive/impulsive symptoms (most common presentations in clinic samples, Willcutt, 2012). Although ADHD, along with all other conditions in the DSM-5, is considered as a diagnostic category (i.e., the disorder is either present or not), there is a broad consensus that ADHD, as well as nearly all forms of psychopathology, is best conceptualized scientifically in dimensional rather than categorical terms (Ahmad & Hinshaw, 2016; Faraone et al., 2015; Hinshaw, 2018; Nigg, 2017; Thapar & Cooper, 2016). Namely, the presentations of ADHD are best understood as representing two distinct, albeit highly-related dimensions of inattention-disorganization and hyperactivity-impulsivity on which individuals differ (Ahmad & Hinshaw, 2016; Faraone et al., 2015; Nigg, 2017a,b; Thapar & Cooper, 2016).[1] Those who are at the extreme end of the dimension, i.e., who are highly inattentive-disorganized and/or hyperactive-impulsive with accompanying impairments have ADHD. In other words, it is the degree to which people with ADHD have trouble sitting still, paying attention, or controlling impulsive behavior that distinguishes them from people without the disorder. Thus, although defining ADHD categorically (DSM-5) is useful given that clinical decisions tend to be categorical in nature (i.e., the individual either does or does not have a disorder that requires treatment),

---

[1] These two dimensions of behavior are almost uniformly found when symptoms of ADHD as rated by parents and teachers are factor-analyzed (Roberts et al., 2015). Factor analysis is a statistical technique used by researches to provide insight into the psychological dimensions (factors) that may account for the relationship among variables in a given data set (McGill & Dombrowski, 2017). In the case of ADHD, numerous factor analyses of the multitude of various symptoms have found that they are manifestations of only two psychological dimensions: attention-disorganization and hyperactivity-impulsivity.

like many medical disorders such as hypertension or diabetes, as well as most mental disorders, ADHD is best understood scientifically as an extreme expression of symptoms (Beauchaine & Klein, 2017; Hinshaw, 2018; Thapar & Cooper, 2016). Also in common with medical disorders, there is an inherent arbitrariness in the assigning of diagnostic thresholds for mental disorders because of the lack of an objective cut-point that defines the diagnostic threshold (Clark, Cuthbert, Lewis-Fernandez, Narrow, & Reed, 2017; Thapar & Cooper, 2016). Thus, many individuals whose ADHD symptoms are just below the cut-point (threshold) for a categorical DSM-5 diagnosis still have symptoms that are sufficiently extreme on either of the inattentive/disorganized or hyperactive/impulsive dimensions to cause significant impairment (Thapar & Cooper, 2016). The DSM recognizes this by providing for subthreshold presentations through the use of NOS (not otherwise specified) diagnoses for many mental disorders, including ADHD (Clark et al., 2017).

In conclusion, ADHD is a clinical disorder marked by developmentally extreme and impairing symptoms of inattention-disorganization and hyperactivity-impulsivity and accompanying impairments in life functioning. The specific manifestations of these symptoms will be discussed along with examples of how the symptoms can increase risk for criminal offending or may be exhibited in criminal justice settings.

Inattention-Disorganization

Attention can be broadly understood as the ability to filter the vast amount of information than surrounds us and to focus on one piece or source of information (Nigg, 2006; 2017a,b). It is multifaceted and mediated by different cognitive processes linked to different brain networks that support the control of attention (Nigg, 2016, 2017b; Posner, Rothbart, & Voelker, 2016). In addition, attention can also be influenced by emotion and motivational processes such level of interest or reward (Nigg, 2006; 2017b). Failure of one or more of these processes can result in impairments in attention. Individuals who are impaired on this dimension have difficulty focusing attention, sustaining the focus, and shifting the focus which can contribute to problems with organization, prioritizing tasks, and time management (Brown, 2013). This can be seen in problems of keeping track of plans, items and time; important items are misplaced or lost (e.g., keys, phones); offices, desks specific rooms in homes can be a messy disaster; there are failures to plan ahead; tardiness for meetings or appointments is common; fees are not paid on time, etc. (Hinshaw & Ellison, 2016; Ramsay, 2015). Interestingly, poor time management may not simply be a function of inattention-disorganization. It may also be due to an inherent, poor sense of time (Nigg, 2017a).

The key diagnostic symptoms of attention-disorganization as detailed in the DSM-5 are presented below. If 6 or more of these symptoms, or 5 or more for those 17 years or older are occurring frequently (i.e., beyond what is considered to be normal)[2] and have persisted for at least 6 months with resultant impairment in functioning, then the individual can be diagnosed with ADHD with a predominantly inattentive presentation (ADHD-PI) or ADHD combined presentation (ADHD-C) if criteria are also met for symptoms of hyperactivity-impulsivity. Diagnostic criteria also specify that impairment from the symptoms must be present in two or more settings (e.g., home, school, work), and cannot be better explained by the presence of another mental disorder. A major limitation of this symptom list is that because it was originally developed for children and adolescents, it may not be sensitive to adult ADHD symptom manifestation (Roberts, Milich, & Barkley, 2015). In an attempt to overcome this limitation, DSM-5 provides examples of how the symptoms might be expressed in late adolescence and adulthood. Although the majority of people who have ADHD have ADHD-PI, most who get diagnosed have ADHD-C since their disruptive, annoying behavior makes it more likely that a parent, teacher, spouse, etc. will notice and/or be affected by the behavior which can result in a referral to a mental health professional (Hinshaw & Ellison, 2016).

The specific DSM-5 symptoms and examples of how these symptoms may be expressed in childhood and late adolescence and adulthood are drawn from the ADHD Child Evaluation diagnostic interview schedule (Young, 2015), examples from the DSM-5, and Ramsay (2015). The child examples will focus on school functioning since it is in a structured setting that the symptoms and impairments tend to be most evident.

- *Does not give close attention to details or makes careless mistakes*
    - **Child:** They may hand in incomplete work and/or poorly presented work that looks rushed and contains many errors. On test papers, children may skip questions and/or not think to

[2] Obviously, a determination of what is "normal" can be a rather subjective judgement. This subjectivity can be substantially overcome through the use of a well-normed rating scales such as the *Connors Rating Scale for Children* (3rd ed.) [Connors, 2008] and the *Barkley Adult ADHD Rating Scale-IV* (Barkley, 2011). Scales such as these enable the diagnostician to compare the behavior of the individual with others of his/her own age and thus to determine how atypical the behavior is.

check whether there are more questions on the other side of the paper. Children may find tasks that require a lot of detail particularly stressful and time consuming.
  - **Adult:** They overlook or miss details, work is inaccurate.
- *Has difficulty in sustaining attention on tasks or play activities*
  - **Child:** They may find tasks that are repetitive and/or require sustained mental effort notably difficult compared to their peers. For example the child may complain and/or struggle with essay based tasks. Teachers may comment that the child needs frequent reminders and redirection to return to the task. The child may state the task is boring and seem to lack the motivation to reach the end, becoming irritable, frustrated and/or disruptive. By contrast, they may struggle less (or not at all) with tasks they enjoy.
  - **Adult:** They have difficulty remaining focused during lectures, conversations, or lengthy reading.
- *Does not seem to listen when directly spoken to*
  - **Child:** Teachers may comment that the child is not listening in class. They may comment that the child requires instructions to be repeated many times and/or broken down into small steps in order to successfully complete a task. Teachers may move the child to sit at the front of the class or next to an assistant. Some teachers may misperceive the child's presentation to be defiant behavior.
  - **Adult:** Their mind seems elsewhere, even in the absence of any obvious distraction.
- *Does not follow through on instructions and does not finish schoolwork, chores, or duties in the workplace*
  - **Child:** They may have difficulty following and remembering instructions, leading to incomplete tasks and unmet goals. For example, the child may be observed to start a practical activity but forget or miss out steps or go off-task and leave it prematurely. Children may receive warnings or detentions for oppositional behavior due to incomplete classwork and homework.
  - **Adult:** They start a task but quickly lose focus, are easily sidetracked.
- *Has trouble organizing task or activities*
  - **Child:** They may miss deadlines as they have not organized or planned their work efficiently. They may appear to be generally messy and untidy (in their appearance and with their

belongings). When the timetable becomes more complicated during the transition to secondary school, children may frequently turn up late for lessons and become stressed by the higher expectation of autonomy. They may leave things behind at home, such as their bus pass, locker key, snack box, sports kit and homework.
  - **Adult:** They have difficulty managing sequential tasks, difficulty keeping materials and belongings in order. Their work is messy, disorganized. They have poor time management, fail to meet deadlines.
- *Avoids, dislikes, or is reluctant to do tasks that need sustained mental effort*
  - **Child:** They may try to avoid specific lessons that they find particularly intensive and require mental effort, such as math, writing and essays. During lessons, the child may protest or lack effort and become frustrated and irritable. They may become restless and/or oppositional.
  - **Adult:** They have difficulty preparing reports, completing forms, reviewing lengthy papers. They procrastinate, tasks are put off until the last minute, need the pressure of deadlines to motivate them. They are aware of task priority but avoid working on it and escape into pleasurable distractions.
- *Loses things needed for tasks or activities*
  - **Child:** They may lose or misplace their school bag, books, school uniform, bus pass and sports kit. The child may often be checking lost property at school to search for lost clothing, pencil cases and school books. Teachers report the child often attends lessons without the equipment or materials required for lessons.
  - **Adult:** They lose tools, wallets, keys, eyeglasses, paperwork, mobile telephones.
- *Easily distracted*
  - **Child:** They may appear to be more distracted by their surroundings than their peers. They may be distracted by noise and activity in the classroom, as well as noise and activity from outside such as children in the playground or any outside sports. Teachers may report that they go off-task because they chatter to peers, or are seen to be daydreaming and require prompting to return to the task. It may be reported that they work better one-to-one or in small groups.

- **Adult:** They are distracted by unrelated thoughts, excessive mind-wandering with multiple unrelated thoughts, jump from one topic to another. They have a difficult time reengaging in a task once focus has been disrupted.

- *Forgetful in daily activities*
  - **Child:** They may regularly forget their timetable and/or leave items at home that they need for class. They may forget to collect all their belongings as they move from classroom to classroom. The child may forget when their homework is due and fail to hand it in on time, even if it has been completed. They may forget to attend meetings and appointments, or even detentions, despite knowing the consequence.
  - **Adult:** They fail to return calls, pay bills, keep appointments

Of all the symptoms of inattention-disorganization, *often easily distracted* and *difficulty sustaining attention* are core symptoms across all age groups (Martel, Levinson, Langer, & Nigg, 2016). Therefore, these two symptoms should be especially focused on in the assessment of inattention. The following vignettes provide examples of *distractibility, disorganization* and *difficulty sustaining attention.*

Distractibility

Imagine that you are sitting in a sixth-grade classroom. The teacher is introducing a new chapter in your social studies book. As she begins to read, all you hear is "the ancient Egyptians" because a passing car catches your eye. It's the same color as your Dad's car. It reminds you of the trip you took the day he brought the new car home. A "breaking-in" drive he had called it.

You hear a few more of the teacher's words, "...pyramids as burial...." You recall a movie you saw with pyramids. "King Tut and thieves," she continues. You imagine all the tunnels inside one of the mammoth structures. You see yourself trapped and hear the blocks sliding as they block the exit.

Again, you hear the teacher's voice, "...took hundreds of years...," and you see a calendar with pages flying off into space. Space brings the image of the solar system spinning and asteroids just missing each other.

"...Paying attention?" You realize the teacher is talking to you. In fact, she is standing right beside you, and the class is snickering. Your mind is

snapped cruelly back to the classroom. You hadn't realized you'd been so far away.

Tom Cradit (2017)

Disorganization

I am horribly disorganized, both at work and at home. I have a tremendously difficult time completing the tasks before me without succumbing to major tangential distractions. I find it nearly impossible to do simple things I know are necessary, from getting to places on time to completing ordinary tasks. My marriage gets strained to near breaking point at times due to my inability to maintain a conversation or project reliably. When I do find something that piques by interest, all else will get pushed aside to make room for it.

Young male adult (Attention, April, 2004)

Sustained attention

If I wasn't deeply interested in a subject, I couldn't concentrate on it at all—those dreadful algebra classes, those Bunsen burners, the mystifying and now deservedly extinct slide rule! Late in each semester, when it became obvious to me that I had no idea what I was supposed to have learned, I'd attend some makeup classes and try desperately to pay attention. As the teacher rattled on, I would grind my teeth, twirl the tops of my socks around my index finger—once I poked myself repeatedly through my pocket with a pin—anything to keep my mind engaged. But it was impossible: a leaf would fall outside the open window, or I'd notice the pattern of the veins on a girl's hand, or a shout from the playground would trigger a set of irresistible associations that carried me back to another day.

Tim Page (2007)

Variability in Sustained Attention

As previously discussed, motivational processes such as level of interest and reward can influence attention. This helps explain the aspect of ADHD that is perhaps least understood by the general public, and what one of the leading experts on ADHD, Thomas Brown (2017), suggests is the "central mystery" of ADHD (p.1). Namely, depending upon the situation, there can be tremendous variation in sustained attention (Roberts et al., 2015). This perplexing feature of ADHD is captured by Nigg (2006) in his authoritative book on the causes of ADHD when he poses the question... "Why can Mary play video games for 2 hours without interruption, when she cannot focus on her homework for 5 minutes (p.

74)?" As the DSM-5 notes, ADHD symptoms may be minimal or absent when the individual is receiving frequent rewards for appropriate behavior, is under close supervision, is in a novel setting, or is engaged in especially interesting activities. Indeed, in situations that the individual finds especially interesting such as playing video games, they may be able to hyperfocus (Hinshaw, 2018). This tremendous variation in sustained attention has prompted Nora Volkow, the director of the National Institute of Drug Abuse in the U.S., to view ADHD as an *interest disorder* (Hinshaw & Ellison, 2016). However, it cannot be emphasized enough that this tremendous variation in sustained attention is not a defect of will power or laziness, but has a strong biological basis that will be addressed in the chapter on causes. It is not due to *won't* but to *can't.* As Tim Page declared in the prior vignette, he truly "couldn't concentrate at all."

Possible Second Attention Disorder

Strong evidence has been accumulating for a set of symptoms distinct from, yet highly related to the inattentive symptoms of ADHD-PI that are possibly indicative of second attention disorder typically termed *Sluggish Cognitive Tempo* (SCT) in the literature (Barkley, 2015b; 2016; Becker, 2017; Becker et al., 2017).[3] Symptoms include "lost in a fog," "stares blankly into space," "daydreams" and have been associated with academic and social impairments, anxiety and depression (Becker et al., 2016; Saez, Servera, Becker, & Burns, 2018). Thus, those with ADHD-PI appear to be a mixed group with perhaps 50% having SCT (Roberts et al., 2015). The following vignette provides an illustration of SCT.

> *For as long as I can remember, I have been a "day-dreamer," sluggish, hypoactive, passive, and most of all, confused. My confusion usually set in because I would be spacing out during the teachers' directions or lecture, so I never knew what I should be doing. High school was especially hard for me, because I honestly do not think I learned anything at all. I always felt lost and academically inadequate, because I did not understand why I never knew what I was doing, and I could never explain what was happening inside my head. I though what I was experiencing was normal until I met with a doctor who prescribed me medication to help with my sluggish, space-cadet symptoms. I started medication my second semester of college and that is when learning became something fascinating and stimulating rather than a burden I was fighting off. I truly believe that I even have an advantage over people who do not take medication, because I*

[3] Barkley (2015b) prefers the designation *Concentration Deficit Disorder* as more accurate and less stigmatizing than SCT.

can focus longer, harder, and remember more information than most people I encounter.

Young male adult (author's case)

Hyperactive-Impulsive

Impulsivity can generally be understood as a "predisposition for rapid, but often premature actions without appropriate foresight" (Dalley & Robbins, 2017, p. 18). Like attention, this broad definition should not be interpreted to mean that impulsivity is a unitary construct. It is multifaceted with different components that underlie different forms of impulsive behavior which are mediated by different psychological processes and brain networks (Cross, Copping, & Campbell, 2011; Dalley & Robbins, 2017; Sharma, Markson, & Clark, 2014). For example, Sharma and colleagues argue for four distinct impulsigenic traits, two of which are most relevant to understanding how ADHD increases risk for criminal offending. One is "sensation-seeking" which can be defined as the seeking of varied, novel, complex, and intense sensations and experiences, and the willingness to take physical, social, legal, and financial risks for the sake of such experiences (Zuckerman, 2007). Sensation seekers do not seek risk for its own sake but are looking for novel and intense sensations and experiences. In their search, however, they are more willing than others to tolerate risk and therefore more likely to enter into risky situations than low sensation seekers (Zuckerman, 2007). The other trait is "disinhibition vs. constraint/ conscientiousness" which reflects impulsive behaviors that arise from lack of planning, or failure to persist in the face of challenges and is strongly related to antisocial behaviors (Sharma et al., 2014). It closely echoes the description in the DSM-5 which specifies that impulsivity is demonstrated by "hasty actions that occur in the moment without forethought and have a high potential for harm to the individual…a desire for immediate rewards or an inability to delay gratification…and/or making important decisions without consideration of long term consequences" (APA, 2013, p. 60). It is this impulsigenic trait that is employed in the theory of Beauchaine and colleagues linking ADHD to criminal behavior (Beauchaine et al., 2017a; Beauchaine, Hinshaw, & Pang, 2010; Beauchaine & McNulty, 2013; Neuhaus & Beauchaine, 2017), and therefore the trait that will be emphasized in this book. The specific DSM-5 symptoms of hyperactivity-impulsivity and examples of how these symptoms might be expressed in childhood and late adolescence and adulthood are based upon the ADHD Child Evaluation diagnostic interview schedule (Young, 2015), examples from the DSM-5, Barkley's ADHD diagnostic criteria (Roberts et al., 2015) for adults, and other sources.

- *Fidget with or taps hands or feet, or squirms in seat*
    - **Child:** Teachers may comment that the child is fidgety and restless in class, irrespective of the topic or activity, and that their fidgeting disturbs other children. The child may shuffle about in their seat, kick their legs, rock back on their chair, fiddle with items on the table, and/or doodle on their books. The child may be perceived as clumsy because they often fall over or knock over items.
    - **Adult:** Overt large motor hyperactivity is replaced with an internal sense of physical and mental restlessness. They exhibit an inability to relax. "You're drumming your fingers, tapping your feet, humming a song, whistling, looking there, stretching, doodling…" (Hallowell & Ratey, 2005, p.6).
- *Leaves seat situations when staying seated is expected*
    - **Child:** Despite frequent reminders and redirection, the child may struggle to stay seated. The child may swing back on their chair or leave their seat and sit on the floor. When engaged in floor work, the child may roll about on the floor and disrupt peers. The child may find excuses to get up and move around, such as to go to the toilet, to go and talk to someone, or to look at something. The child may be unable to modify their behavior, even when redirected or reprimanded.
    - **Adult:** They leave their seat in the office, other workplace, or in other situations that require remaining in place.
- *Runs about or climbs when not appropriate*
    - **Child:** They may appear restless and eager for break time and physical activities when they can engage in boisterous play and climbing activities. They may need time to calm down when returning to the classroom. The child may be reprimanded for running in corridors. On class trips they may need additional supervision to ensure they stay with the group or walk safely. Older children may appear more restless and fidgety than overtly active.
    - **Adult:** Their overt hyperactivity exhibited in childhood diminishes and is replaced by an inner restlessness.
- *Unable to play or undertake leisure activities quietly*
    - **Child:** They may talk or shout when it's quiet time or during activities that require concentration. They may ask lots of

questions, talk over others, and distract their peers. Reminders to be quiet and/or reprimands don't seem to help. Given the choice, the child may avoid quiet activities, preferring to choose physically active or noisy ones.
    - **Adult:** They have difficulty relaxing, feel restless, search for high stimulation.
- *"On the go," acts as if "driven by a motor"*
    - **Child:** The child may be a whirlwind, running, climbing, and moving aimlessly between activities. The child may appear to be always on the go. At the end of the day the child may not seem to be tired but instead presents as irritable or overwhelmed. The child may favor anticipated break times and physical activities rather than class work. Given the choice, extra-curricular activities involve physical activities rather than less active pursuits.
    - **Adult:** They must constantly being doing something, are unability to relax, do not fully engage, e.g., always on electronic device, even in the company of others.
- *Talks excessively*
    - **Child:** They may chatter to peers in class, even when they have been asked to work quietly or during tests. They may not respond to reminders or reprimands.
    - **Adult:** They may dominate conversations, talk over others, and give tangential responses to questions.
- *Blurts out answers before a question has been finished*
    - **Child:** They may be frequently reminded or reprimanded for talking in lessons. The child may seem to dominate the class by frequently calling out or talking over others. The child may have difficulty waiting for their turn to speak and/or answer questions.
    - **Adult:** They may struggle to follow the 'turn-taking' rules of conversation but instead seem motivated to say immediately what is on their mind (even if this is unrelated to the topic of conversation). They may seem to be impatient for others to finish speaking. They may finish other people's sentences for them.
- *Has difficulty waiting his or her turn*
    - **Child:** They may be reprimanded for queue jumping and/or not taking turns in class activities or when playing with friends. The child may appear to be oppositional and/or become distressed or

agitated, even for activities that require a short wait and/or waiting for a desired activity
- o **Adult:** They tend to be highly impatient waiting in lines, traffic, etc. In a car they may have only one gear: fast forward.

- *Interrupts or intrudes on others*
  - o **Child:** Teachers may notice that the child tends to interrupt others, speak out in assembly, use things that do not belong to them, and/or appear to monopolize and take over the personal space and time of others (both children and staff).
  - o **Adult:** They tend to be over-talkative, interrupting, speaking too loudly.

The following vignettes provide more elaborate examples of the core symptoms of hyperactivity and impulsivity.

Hyperactivity

Essentially, I feel like I need to be in constant motion or I will explode! Overall, it seems my energy level is sometimes inexhaustible. I avoid activities that require me to be quiet. When I participate in activities that do require me to be quiet, it seems like a death sentence to me. I have always been a talker. I can talk about absolutely nothing, with anyone, forever! I have been a chatterbox ever since I was about five. You would think by now I would have run out of things to say. –

Young adult male (author's case)

My parents say that I was hyperactive from the day I could walk. I really didn't spend much time crawling. I guess I thought it was too slow. Once I started walking, I got into everything. I'd take stuff out of drawers, closets, cabinets, etc., throw the stuff on the floor, and then move on to the next thing that caught by eye.

When I got a little older, I loved climbing trees. When I wasn't climbing, I was running. My parents had to restrain me in parking lots or street corners, as I would have run out into traffic.

Young adult male (author's case)

Impulsivity

I was only nine years old but, boy, do I remember the incident. My father and his friend came back from skin diving and left their spears at the front of the caravan. I grabbed my dad's Hawaiian sling to show cousin Lachlan how it worked, shooting it vertically about ten meters into the air. I repeated this a number of times, until a strong gust of wind blew the spear onto the power lines. It short-circuited the two wires. This happened all in a blink of an eye.

The power pole that Lachlan and I were standing under exploded, with sparks flying everywhere. The current then flowed through all the other poles, blowing them up one after the other in a circle around the caravan park. Every power line connected between the poles fell to the ground, just missing tents and caravans.

People came running to see what had happened. I don't know how it was that no one was killed or injured. The only wires that did not fall were the two with the aluminum spear still lying across them. A State Electricity Commission team arrived to repair the damage.

Young adult male (Polis, 2003, p. 34)

Many of us with ADHD crave high-stimulus situations. In my case, I love casinos and horse races. Obviously, a craving for high stimulation can get a person into trouble, which is why ADHD is prevalent among criminals and self-destructive risk-takers.

Hallowell & Ratey (2005, p. 25)

Emotional Impulsivity

From the first medical description of ADHD in 1775, and for 193 years thereafter, deficiencies in emotional dysregulation manifested in symptoms of impulsive emotion and poor control of emotion were viewed as central to ADHD (Barkley, 2015c, 2016b). Then, "inexplicably" (Barkley, 2016a, p. 249) these symptoms were dropped for the second edition of the DSM in 1968 and subsequent versions, being relegated to the status of commonly occurring associated symptoms, not core symptoms. However, in the past 2 decades, Russell Barkley (2015c, 2016b) has been contending that symptoms of emotional impulsivity are core symptoms of ADHD. "Those with ADHD will be as impulsive with their primary emotions as they are with their motor or behavior responses because they are essentially a single unitary action: Action and emotion are united in the response" (Barkley, 2015c, p. 88). Emotional impulsivity is manifested in low frustration tolerance, impatience, quickness to anger, and being easily excited to emotional reactions more generally. Barkley's position has received support from a recent meta-analysis of 77 studies, including more than 32,000 youth, which provided evidence for the central role of emotion dysregulation problems in ADHD (Graziano & Garcia, 2016). Adults with ADHD-C also frequently exhibit symptoms of emotional dysregulation (Adler et al., 2016; Asherson et al., 2016). Karalunas and colleagues (2014), in a study of 437 community-recruited children with and without ADHD, have proposed three novel subtypes of childhood ADHD using temperamental dimensions. In the subtype labeled *irritability,* children in addition to symptoms of impulsivity and attentional dyscontrol exhibited extreme levels of negative emotionality, anger, and poor soothability. Similarly, Petrovic and Castellanos (2016) have proposed an emotional type of ADHD which lies intermediate on a gradient of clinical conditions without an inherent emotional component such as ADHD-PI to conditions of extreme emotional instability such as bipolar disorder. Thus, "the link between ADHD and emotion-related dysfunction is increasingly well-established" (Musser & Nigg, 2017, p. 1).

However, Barkley's position is by no means universally endorsed. For example, Theodore Beauchaine (2015), while acknowledging that symptoms of emotional impulsivity are common among those with ADHD (the position of DSM-5), views these symptoms not as core symptoms but as symptoms arising primarily from deficient socialization practices in families of children with ADHD. These practices can be partly influenced by behavioral impulsivity in the case of ADHD. Thus, emotional impulsivity rather than being a symptom intrinsic to ADHD is acquired "through negative reinforcement processes that occur thousands of times across development in at risk families and peer groups, and through recurrent stress that occurs early in life" (Beauchaine (2015, p. 883).

Although it is neither within the scope of this book nor the competence of the author to resolve the controversy, perhaps Joel Nigg, one of the pre-eminent research scientists in ADHD, has it right when he reported the following in a personal communication (2/22/2018) to the author. "I don't exactly agree with Russ or Ted's formulation. I am increasingly thinking in terms of breakdowns in the self-regulation system(s) that manifest as very different forms of ADHD—some of these forms have major problems in emotion regulation; but others do not. So to challenge Russ, I would say we have kids with ADHD without emotion regulation problems, and some who do—that means emotion regulation is extremely important in ADHD, but not inevitably a major feature. To challenge Ted, I would say what do you do with the child who is emotionally dysregulated and difficult to manage from birth and never regulates, and never can be managed, no matter how skilled the parental socialization. And why are socialization practices in ADHD families often perfectly normal" (communication was excerpted and abbreviated).

It would seem that one key to the resolution of the controversy would be to determine the age of onset of emotional dysregulation symptoms.

The Beauchaine position would suggest that such symptoms typically do not occur in individuals with ADHD until childhood or later. However, if the Barkley formulation is correct, or the Nigg modification that at least for some children emotional dysregulation is a core feature, then the age onset should be seen as early as preschool. Evidence supporting an early manifestation of emotional dysregulation comes from studies in which it is clear that that an accurate diagnosis of ADHD can be made in this age period (Lahey et al. 2016) and that preschool children can manifest signs of emotional dysregulation such as abnormal irritability (Wakschlag et al., 2018). Additional evidence comes from a longitudinal study of 161 children aged 3-4 years (96 diagnosed with ADHD) which found that negative emotionality/anger diagnosed in preschool predicted ADHD symptom severity at age 7 (Rabinovitz, O'Neill, Rajendram, & Halperin, 2016). Also, a recent large-scale analyzing 1713 individuals with ADHD and 1529 controls, Hoogman and colleagues (2017) found reduced volume in brain regions involved in emotional regulation in individuals with ADHD which they interpreted as supporting the inclusion of emotional regulation as a core symptom of ADHD. As Lugo-Candelas and Posner (2017, p. 267) noted, this finding if replicated by future studies, is of "enormous consequence to our conceptualization of the disorder…. as it will require the neuroscience field to decide whether ADHD should continue to be understood as a purely cognitive disorder, or should also be examined through the lens of a mood disorder."

In conclusion, this issue is not simply an arid academic dispute but is of "enormous consequence" especially for the role ADHD plays as a risk factor for criminal behavior. It is widely accepted that problems with emotional dysregulation confer significant risk not only for a wide range of psychopathology in general (Beauchaine, 2015; McLaughlin, 2017) but for aggressive and criminal behavior in particular (DeLisi & Vaughn, 2014; Garofalo & Wright, 2017). If indeed emotional impulsivity is a core feature for some individuals with ADHD on a par with behavioral impulsivity, then the risk ADHD poses for criminal behavior for these individuals is greatly increased. Thus, given the widespread consensus that symptoms of emotional dysregulation are prevalent in ADHD throughout the life span and are major contributors to impairments (Shaw, Stringaris, Nigg, & Leibenluft, 2014), emotional dysregulation (whether intrinsic to ADHD or acquired) markedly increases the risk ADHD poses for the development of antisocial behavior, as will subsequently be discussed.

Prevalence

Prevalence refers to the proportion of individuals in the general population, or specific populations (e.g., incarcerated individuals), who have a disorder such as ADHD. There is an enormous literature (mostly based on juveniles) attempting to provide reliable general population estimates of ADHD that is based on two major methodologies (Hinshaw, 2018; Hinshaw & Ellison, 2016; Roberts et al., 2015; Sayal, Prasad, Daley, Ford, & Coghill, 2018). The first method identifies *diagnostic prevalence* which refers to the percentage of individuals who report having received a diagnosis from a mental health professional. For example, in the U.S. the most recent data of the prevalence of ADHD in juveniles (aged 2-17) comes from the United States of America National Survey of Children's Health conducted in 2016 in which parents were asked if a "doctor or other health provider ever told you that [child] had attention deficit disorder or attention-deficit/hyperactivity disorder, that is, ADD, or ADHD" (Danielson et al., 2018).[4] The prevalence of ever having received such a diagnosis was 9.4% (12.9% male, 5.6% female). This represents a 41% increase from 2003 (Hinshaw, 2018). The prevalence of a current diagnosis of ADHD was 8.4% overall (11.5% male, 5.1% female). These diagnoses may or may not have been accurate. As with prevalence estimates of most mental disorders (Wolpert & Ford, 2015), estimates based upon this method can result in underreporting or overreporting. Underreporting can occur because parents lack access to qualified mental health practitioners to conduct an evaluation. Overreporting, which is by far the more likely occurrence given the surging rates (i.e., 41% increase from 2003 to 2012 in the U.S.) of diagnostic prevalence among juveniles, can be caused by a number of factors having largely to do with educational practices and policies that have incentivized an ADHD diagnosis (Hinshaw, 2018). An additional factor of no small importance is the use of "cursory diagnostic procedures in many locales" (Hinshaw & Ellison, 2016, p. 19) which can be as risibly brief as 15 minutes (Hinshaw & Scheffler, 2014). These factors suggest that the 9.4% rate overstates the true prevalence of ADHD (Hinshaw, 2018).

The second method identifies *population prevalence* which refers to the percentage of individuals in a general or specific population who have ADHD. This method has two components. First, a sample of individuals is drawn from the general population based upon random sampling

---

[4] Children in the US with ADHD are most commonly diagnosed by pediatricians or other primary care physicians (53%) [Danielson et al., 2018].

techniques that ensure that the individuals are representative of the population in question. Second, for juveniles, parent and/or teacher rating scales are used to identify ADHD symptoms. In addition to such measures, trained interviewers conduct clinical interviews for ADHD symptoms (Roberts et al., 2015). For adults, the method typically relies exclusively on a clinical interview without any input from collateral informants who might know the individual quite well such as a parent, spouse, close friend, etc. Although international prevalence rates for juveniles vary widely from region to region, the results of numerous studies suggest that there is little variation in true prevalence once differences in measurement factors are taken into account. Systematic reviews indicate that population prevalence globally is between 5% and 7%, with males approximately 2½ times more likely than girls to have ADHD (Nigg, 2017a; Hinshaw, 2018; Polanczyk, Willcutt, Salum, Kieling, & Rohde, 2014; Sayal, Prasad, Ford, & Coghill, 2018; Thomas, Sanders, Doust, Beller, & Glasziou, 2015; Willcutt, 2012). This global rate, which is based upon standardized diagnostic procedures rather than cursory assessments, has not changed in the past three decades (Polanczyk et al., 2014). Similarly, in the U.S., although diagnostic prevalence of youth ADHD has increased in the past two decades, ADHD-related symptoms have not (Safer, 2018). Thus, there does not appear to have been any actual large increase in the true prevalence of ADHD comparable to the increased rates based upon diagnostic prevalence of ADHD (Hinshaw, 2018).

For adults, the most current population prevalence study of ADHD in the U.S. used a nationally representative sample of 3,199 18-44-year old adults who were initially screened for ADHD using a lay-administered diagnostic interview followed by blinded clinical interviews for those who screened positive by doctoral-level psychologists (Kessler et al., 2006). The study reported a current prevalence of ADHD of 4.4% (3.2% female, 5.4% male) which is relatively similar to the global prevalence of adult ADHD (Roberts et al., 2015). However, this prevalence is most likely an underestimate for several reasons.

First, and most importantly, in contrast to studies of child population prevalence of ADHD, in studies of ADHD population prevalence in adults there was no input from collateral informants. The importance of collateral informants cannot be overestimated since exclusive reliance on self-report can lead to a vast underreporting of ADHD symptom severity in young adults (Barkley, 2016; Molina & Sibley, 2014). For example, the Milwaukee longitudinal study of child clinic cases of ADHD (n=158) who were followed up into young adulthood (age 21) found only 4% who were diagnosed with ADHD in childhood reported enough current symptoms to qualify for a DSM-IV diagnosis of ADHD (Barkley, Murphy, & Fischer, 2008). However, use of parent report on the same criteria found that a "whopping 10 times more still met criteria for the disorder" (i.e., 46%) (Barkley, 2016, p. 7). The reliability of the parent-report over the adult self-report in providing an estimate of current ADHD symptoms was supported by its far greater association with various concurrent measures of impairment (Barkley et al., 2008). Similarly, in the most recent follow-up (age 25) of the landmark Multimodal Treatment Study of children with ADHD (MTA),[5] there was a vast discrepancy between self and parent-reported ADHD symptoms, with parent-reported symptoms being 40-137% higher than self-report (depending upon the number of factors used to classify cases) and correlating well with functional outcomes (Roy & Hechtman, 2017; Sibley et al., 2017).

Second, the prevalence rate was based on the older DSM-IV rather than the more sensitive DSM-5 criteria. This has been shown to underestimate the prevalence in adolescents and adults. Vande Voort, He, Jameson, and Merikangas (2014) compared the prevalence of DSM-IV versus DSM-5 ADHD in a nationally representative sample of 1,894 participants 12 to 15 years of age in which trained lay interviewers conducted a structured interview with parents. The study found an increase in prevalence from 7.38% to 10.84% (14.10 male; 7.57 female). The children whose onset was between ages of 7 and 12 years were not systematically different in terms of severity and comorbidity when compared to children whose onset occurred before the age of 7 years. A study of adults which pooled the results of two general population surveys in the United States reported a prevalence rate of 8.2% (approximately the same for both males and females) based on DSM-5 criteria (Ustan et al., 2017). This finding is almost double the 4% prevalence reported just over

[5] The MTA is the largest treatment study to date with the most representative, generalizable clinical sample of children with ADHD (McGough, 2016). The initial purpose of the study was to establish specific treatment strategies and to assess the effectiveness of such strategies. To this end, the participants (579 children, 465 males diagnosed with ADHD-C at ages 7-9) were recruited from a variety of sources (e.g., mental health centers, advertisements, pediatric referrals) and randomly assigned to 4 groups: (1) medication management, (2) behavior therapy, (3) medication and behavior therapy, (4) community care, of whom approximately 2/3's were treated with medication. At the study's end at 14 months the subjects returned to various forms of community care. It was also decided to extend the study in terms of various follow-ups with the most recent being at a mean age of 25.

10 years ago by the same group using similar approaches (Kessler et al., 2006; Shaw, Ahn, & Rapoport, 2017).

Third, since the DSM symptoms were based upon childhood manifestations of ADHD presentations, it is unclear whether the symptom set is developmentally appropriate for late adolescents or young adults (Roberts et al., 2015; Sibley & Kuriyan, 2016). Thus, the documented decline of symptoms (especially hyperactivity/impulsivity) may be due to the lack of sensitivity of the DSM criteria rather than a true decline (Roberts et al., 2015). DSM-5 clearly acknowledges this problem and tries to address it by providing descriptions of how the symptoms might be expressed in older teens and adults. However, with the exception of a study of adolescents with ADHD which found that the new descriptors increased by one the total number of ADHD inattentive symptoms endorsed by parents (Sibley & Kuriyan, 2016), the extent to which the descriptors enhance diagnostic accuracy has not been tested (Roberts et al., 2015). Interestingly, Sibley and Kuriyan (2016, p. 184) commented that new DSM-5 descriptors "may partially arrest the noted symptom decline in adolescence." In addition to concerns about the content of the DSM items, it is also questionable whether a cutoff score of five is the best suited to identify an impairing level of ADHD symptoms. Research has shown that a norm-based cutoff[6] score of 4 identifies adults who have functional impairments and therefore the use of a cutoff of 5 will miss adults with impairing ADHD symptoms (Roberts et al., 2015).

In conclusion, the implications for the criminal justice system of the discussion of prevalence are as follows. First, although as with all studies of the prevalence of mental disorders in the general population (Wolpert & Ford, 2015), we do not have a perfectly accurate estimate of the true prevalence of ADHD (juvenile or adult) in the general population, there is no doubt that ADHD is a common problem for males (Nigg, 2017a). Therefore, ADHD is likely to be a common problem among male offenders. Second, and most importantly, if individuals with ADHD in the correctional system are to be accurately identified, it is imperative, if at all possible, to obtain information from collateral informants. Third, the developmental insensitivity of the DSM and ICD symptoms to the manifestations of adult ADHD require that an evaluation for ADHD be conducted by a mental health professional who is well-versed in the common manifestations of adult ADHD that are not captured by the official criteria.

[6] A norm-based cut-off is a cut-off based on the presence of elevated ADHD symptomatology or impairment when compared to control-group norms.

New Understanding of ADHD

The past two decades have brought about a major change in understanding the nature of ADHD (Barkley, 2015d; Brown, 2013; Nigg, 2017b). Whereas previously the focus had been on the symptoms of ADHD, a new deeper and broader understanding has emerged. ADHD is now widely conceptualized as a disorder of self-regulation/self-control[7] (Barkley, 2015d; Brown, 2013; Nigg, 2016, 2017a,b). Indeed, Nigg (2016, p. 593) has declared ADHD to be "paradigmatic of problems in the domain of self-regulation" (SR). SR means the "capacity to optimize our behavior, thinking, and attention, and emotional experience and expression" (Nigg, 2017a, p. 12). It involves not only the ability to control attention, behavior and emotions so that they are adaptive to the situation, but also the ability to activate and persist when needed. There is a consensus that SR involves at least three major components: *alertness/detection, information filtering/accumulation,* and *deliberate control* (Diamond, 2013; Nigg, 2017a,b).

Alertness is the capacity to detect a signal from the environment. For some individuals with ADHD a deficiency in alertness/detection can cause them to seem like they aren't listening or paying attention. They have an underaroused or "sleepy" brain which diminishes their level of alertness (Nigg, 2017a).

Filtering occurs when we need to concentrate to sift through the vast amount of information than surrounds us and to focus on one piece or source of information. There is also another kind of filtering that happens more automatically and all the time (Nigg, 2017b). For example, how are we to process a surprising comment a stranger might make? In an instant, the brain samples the comment and compares it to accumulated information. Individuals with ADHD seem to check and accumulate information more inefficiently or slowly. This slow processing speed is a common finding in ADHD (Willcutt, 2015) which "makes it difficult to rapidly filter incoming information and make good decisions about the appropriate response in many day-to-day situations" (Nigg, 2017b, p. 25).

Deliberately taking control and acting follows upon detection and filtering/accumulation of information (Nigg, 2017b). Deliberate control is

---

[7] Self-regulation and self-control are typically used interchangeably in the literature, as they will be in this book (Nigg, 2017c). Although these constructs are of central importance in psychology, their discussion is characterized by considerable "conceptual clutter" (Nigg, 2017c, p.362). See Nigg (2017c) for a tour de force effort to provide clarity to the variety of terms under which self-regulation/control are discussed.

enabled by several cognitive functions commonly designated executive functions (EFs) [Nigg, 2017a,b]. These include: *response inhibition* (resisting the temptation to act impulsively), *interference control* (resisting internal or external attentional distraction), *cognitive flexibility* (seeing a problem from two different angles or changing task set in relation to a rule or goal), and *working memory* (maintaining information on line) [Diamond, 2013; Engle, 2018l; Nigg, 2017c]. Attentional control is a critical component of working memory (Baddeley, 2012; Engle, 2018). As Engle (2018) noted in a recent article in which he revisited his earlier work: "I now think that the tasks used to measure working memory capacity largely reflect an ability to maintain information in the maelstrom of divergent thought" (p. 192).

To summarize then, ADHD is best conceptualized as a "global self-regulation disorder" (Nigg, 2017a, p. 17) characterized by multiple deficits in the components of SR (Willcutt, 2015). This conceptualization represents a shift away from attempting to identify a single deficit that is necessary and sufficient to cause ADHD to models that posit several deficits. ADHD symptoms and related impairments are thought to arise from the additive or interactive effect of these deficits (Willcutt, 2015). Since a dysfunction can occur in one or more of the components of SR, this helps explain how variations in ADHD occurs. There are ongoing attempts to parse this variation by identifying distinct neuropsychological subtypes of ADHD (e.g., Roberts, Martel, & Nigg, 2017). In short, ADHD is not a "one-size-fits-all-condition" (Nigg, 2017a, p. 37).

Self-Regulation Deficits and the Link to Criminal Offending

Voluminous research has established that impaired SR is of "almost unparalleled importance to mental health" (Nigg, 2017a, p. 661) and may be the single most important variable in explaining the developmental origins of antisocial behavior (Moffitt, 2012; Moffitt et al., 2011). Numerous studies have shown that impaired SR is linked to juvenile and adult criminal behavior (DeLisi, 2015; DeLisi & Vaughn, 2014; Mohr-Jensen, 2016; Vazsonyi, Milkuska, & Kelley, 2017), and it has been shown to be more important than socioeconomic status or IQ in predicting crime (Poulton, Moffitt, & Silva, 2015). Indeed, the importance of impaired SR theory is such that it has been proclaimed the Tyrannosaurus rex of criminology that is poised to devour criminal justice theorizing (De Lisi, 2011). "In terms of empirical tests of its theoretical ideas, citations, influence on the field, self-control theory is "peerless" (DeLisi, 2011, p.

103). Thus, given that ADHD is best understood as "global self-regulation disorder" (Nigg, 2017a, p. 17) and is "paradigmatic of problems in the domain of self-regulation" (Nigg, 2016, p. 593), it follows that ADHD should be a major risk factor for criminal offending. The evidence supporting this conclusion will be reviewed in a subsequent chapter. At this juncture, it is sufficient to provide a few examples to illustrate some of the ways deficits in self-regulation manifested in symptoms of inattention-disorganization and hyperactivity-impulsivity can increase risk for criminal behavior, or may manifest in a criminal justice setting.

Inattention-Disorganization

The most important link of inattention-disorganization to criminal offending is indirect through its adverse impact on school and occupational functioning which in turn increases the risk for criminal offending (Cordova & Wilson, 2017; Farrington, 2012). This link will be discussed in detail in a subsequent chapter. The direct effects of inattention-disorganization can be seen in criminal justice settings where problems with attention may present during interrogations, interviews, or court appearances when the person does not respond to questions and requests. Those with ADHD may miss questions, ask the police officer, attorney, or judge to repeat the question, appear to be daydreaming, appear unconcerned or uncooperative. For example,

> *Jim is a 32-year-old man arrested overnight for a third offense driving under the influence of alcohol. He has sobered up before his court appearance in front of the judge in the morning and has had a chance to assess his situation. He realizes the problems he is facing with not only the law but also with his wife and family, his work, and his finances. He has been through alcohol substance abuse treatment before and knows he will have to do more.*
>
> *In front of the judge he pleads not guilty, and the judge is telling him a number of things of importance that Jim should be totally focused on. Among these are reporting to the probation office as a term of pre-trial release supervision that has been imposed on him, going to a substance abuse treatment facility for an updated substance abuse evaluation, not driving, and attending upcoming court dates. The judge hands him a stack of documents, which Jim takes from him.*
>
> *The problem is that Jim has been trying to listen and think about his mess at the same time. Even though the information is written down for him to*

look at later, Jim heard little of what the judge has explained to him and fails to follow up on the substance abuse evaluation or reporting to the probation officer for pre-trial supervision. He gets released from jail and sets an appointment with his usual lawyer for two weeks down the road. By the time he meets with his lawyer, who asks if he has reported to the probation officer or gotten his substance abuse evaluation, Jim is probably already in even more trouble.

One of Patrick Hurley's cases

Offenders with ADHD-induced deficits in organization and working memory can fail to keep appointments, chronically procrastinate, seem unable to set priorities, and therefore can appear indifferent to requirements and rules placed on them by police, attorneys, parole officers, or judges. For example,

Kyle a personable 20-year-old who was convicted of writing bad checks had a number of problems after being placed on probation. He had been diagnosed at age 10 with ADHD and was on medication and doing better till around age 16 when he decided he no longer wanted to take his medication.

During the pre-trial process his attorney had been frustrated at Kyle's missing appointments and court appearances. Kyle would often show up a day early for a court appearance or a day late for an appointment with his attorney. Consequently, Kyle had created a number of obstacles for his attorney in bargaining with the Prosecutor and Judge for a lighter sentence.

Kyle's probation officer reported similar issues with Kyle. He would come in two days early for his appointment and be frustrated that he was there at the wrong time and when told of his actual appointment time and date he would apologize and leave. Two days later he would be a "no show" for the appointment. His probation officer likes Kyle but states that he seems to be a paradox of being able to do some things well and unable to do other similar things at all. He is supposed to do 100 hours of community service and after six months on probation and having signed up with an organization has completed only four hours. Because of these seemingly minor issues of missing appointments and lack of progress on community service Kyle may be going back to court soon on a recommendation to spend five days in jail for contempt of court.

One of Patrick Hurley's cases

Hyperactivity-Impulsivity

Hyperactive-Impulsive symptoms pose the greatest risk for criminal offending (Beauchaine et al., 2017). Because of their behavioral and emotional impulsivity, individuals with ADHD often have grave difficulty in stopping themselves from doing things that land them in all sorts of trouble, from injuries to serious antisocial behavior. For example, this means that such individuals tend to act without sufficient reflection, are more concerned with the immediate thrill or rewards of their actions rather than the consequences, and only later realize what a mess they have gotten themselves into. The following vignettes illustrate how easily such behaviors can lead to problematic behavior, even in individuals who are otherwise very well socialized, as can been seen in the first two examples.

Even as a young child, I was impulsive and unstoppable. At five, I ran out onto a busy street and was hit by a car, although luckily, I wasn't seriously injured.

Later that year, I was burning some trash with my brother. I decided it would be a good idea to burn the frayed white material from the worn-down knees of my jeans. My pants caught fire. I ended up in the hospital with large burn blisters on both legs.

At 14, I was playing with matches and gasoline in our family's two-car detached garage. The gas can suddenly burst into flames, and the garage burned to the ground with my parent's new car inside. My parents somehow believed the story I made up to cover the incident, although the fire department and several of my siblings were suspicious of my tale. Even then, in early adolescence, I somehow knew that unless I changed my behavior ***I would probably end up in jail someday****.*

One of Patrick Hurley's cases

Even by the age of 2, the one trait that has perhaps most characterized my success had become apparent: TAKING RISKS! I don't remember anything about the incident but, I am told that I almost drowned as a result of an encounter with a high diving board. In later life, one of my mentors joked that I liked to do high dives into empty pools.

As I grew up, more evidence emerged that risk-taking was in my blood. We often played on the railroad tracks. One game involved putting your ear to the rails to see who could remain listening longest after the first tiny vibrations signaled that a train was approaching. As I got older, around age seven, our adventures became more daring, and we began to jump on the freight cars as they passed by. This is not as easy as it sounds for a small boy, even with a slow-moving train, and often a conductor in the caboose would yell and chase us off.

Rebellious and disobedient, I was constantly in trouble during my freshman year and more often than not grounded or in detention. My mother would sometimes check my arms for needle marks. On one occasion, I snuck away from my family to hang out with my friends under the bleachers, where they drank beer and smoked. The gang left the stadium and I found myself in the back seat of a stolen car that was being hot-wired. We set out on a joy ride. When a police car began to follow with flashing lights and siren, I panicked. We swerved into an alley close to the stadium and braked hard. I got out and ran as fast as I could back to the bleachers, my family and a normal life. However adventurous I might be, ***I WAS NOT A CRIMINAL****.*

Craig Venter (2007). Craig Venter headed one of the two teams that decoded the human genome and is the first person ever to have his own genome fully decoded and published.

My son was formally diagnosed as ADHD when he was 5 years old. The psychiatrist told me he was one of the most severe cases he had seen. He is now 27 and incarcerated, serving out probation violations that started with minor traffic fines. But more seriously, he was recently indicted and is facing trial for statutory rape (a 16-year-old daughter of a drug addict). Apparently, he was staying at their house (with the mother's consent-she is a crack-head) and when he finally ran out of money to help support the mom's habit, she (after 11 months) turned him in for statutory rape. He knows the potential legal consequences of messing with 'jail bait', but like so many others with ADHD, ***HE DOESN'T THINK THINGS THROUGH!***

Mother's letter to author

CHAPTER TWO

ETIOLOGY

ADHD is caused by a complex interplay between genetic and environmental (primarily biological) risk factors, and therefore no single cause is either necessary or sufficient to explain its occurrence (Barkley, 2015e; Faraone et al., 2015; Nigg, 2017a,b;Thapar & Cooper, 2016). These risk factors adversely affect the functioning of several brain networks and lead to deficits in various neuropsychological processes which result in the core ADHD symptoms and a wide range of functional impairments (Faraone et al., 2015). As a thorough examination of the multiple factors involved in the etiology (i.e., causes) of ADHD would require a book in itself, a brief review of the core findings will suffice to support the validity of ADHD as a real disorder as well as provide a basic understanding of the etiological complexity of ADHD. Genetic factors will be discussed first, followed by a discussion of environmental factors.

Genetic Factors

"Far and away the most significant contributor" to the etiology of ADHD is genetics (Barkley, 2017, p. 8). Genetic effects can occur in many ways. I will review the most important as identified by Barkley (2017).

Inheritance

As with all psychiatric disorders with significant genetic influences, what is inherited is a combination of a number of genes acting in concert that generate what is variously termed a 'liability' or 'susceptibility' or 'vulnerability' to a disorder such as ADHD (Nigg, 2018). This liability is then thought to interact with certain environmental risk factors (primarily biological in the case of ADHD) to trigger the disorder (Hinshaw, 2018). The evidence for the inheritance of a liability that increases the risk for ADHD is as follows.

It has long been known that ADHD, like many disorders, runs in families or in genetic terms "breeds true." Parents and siblings of individuals with ADHD show between a fivefold and a tenfold increased risk of developing ADHD compared with the general population (Faraone et al., 2015). This results in 25-35% of parents of ADHD children having ADHD, and 25-50% of siblings of children with ADHD having ADHD. In the case of identical twins, if one twin has ADHD, then 70-92% of the time the other twin has the disorder (Barkley, 2017). Most recently Chen and colleagues (2017) demonstrated that the closer the genetic relationship an individual has with a relative who has ADHD the greater the risk for the individual. The increased risk for ADHD was measured by hazard ratios (HRs). An HR is the probability that a relative of an ADHD-affected individual will have ADHD compared to the probability of ADHD in a relative of unaffected individual. For example, a HR of 3 means that a relative of an individual with ADHD is three times more likely to have ADHD than a comparable relative of an individual without ADHD. A HR of 1 means there is no increased risk. The HRs found in the study were as follows: 70.45 for identical twins; 8.44 for fraternal twins; 8.27 for full siblings; 2.86 for maternal half siblings; 2.31 for paternal half siblings; 2.24 for full cousins; 1.47 for half cousins. Thus, having decisively established that family aggregation of ADHD increases with genetic relatedness, the question then becomes how much of this increased risk is due to genetic inheritance versus common family experiences? Numerous twin, family and adoption studies designed to disentangle genetic causes from environmental causes have established that most of the risk is due to genetic inheritance (Nigg, 2016). Namely, about 74% of the variation[1] in the dimensions of inattention-disorganization and hyperactivity-impulsivity for both children and adults is due to variation in the genes the individual inherits from their parents (Faraone & Larsson, 2018). Furthermore, in clinically diagnosed cases, heritability approaches 90% (Hinshaw, 2018). The influence of genes on ADHD is far greater than in major depression, comparable to that for schizophrenia and bipolar

[1] The technical term for this in the discipline of behavioral genetics is *heritability*. Heritability refers to the proportion of phenotypic difference among individuals that can be attributed to genetic differences (Knopik, Neiderhiser, DeFries, & Plomin, 2017). Phenotype refers to the observable characteristics—both physical (e.g., height) and behavioral (e.g. impulsivity)—of an individual. Note that heritability does not refer to the phenotype of a single individual, but to the genetic contribution to differences among individuals on a phenotype. For example, the heritability for height is about 90%, but this does not mean that an individual grew to 90% of his/her height for reasons of heredity and that the other inches were added by the environment. It means that most of the difference in height among individuals is due to the genetic differences among them (Knopik et al., 2017).

disorder, and approaching that of autism spectrum disorders (Barkley, 2017; Hinshaw, 2018; Thapar & Cooper, 2016).

The child inherits many genes (polygenetic) each of which makes a small contribution to overall risk. Cumulatively they increase the risk with more risk genes inherited, the greater the risk. This is designated an *additive* genetic mechanism in behavioral genetics, i.e., the independent effects of genes "add up" to influence a phenotypic characteristic (Knopik et al., 2017). The strong tendency of those with ADHD to marry (mate) with one another (.45 correlation) [Nordsletten et al., 2016] increases the likelihood that their children will inherit a liability for ADHD. The genetic risk variants are identified through *genome wide association studies* (GWAS).[2] However, of the hundreds or perhaps thousands of commonly occurring gene variants involved in ADHD (Faraone & Larsson, 2018; Nigg, 2017b), each making a small contribution to overall risk, the results from studies attempting to identify specific genes and to quantify each gene's contribution to the heritability of ADHD have been "disappointingly small" (Nigg, 2016 p 415), as very few genes having been identified (Cortese, 2016). For example, in the most recent and largest study to date, compelling evidence was found for just 12 genes (Demontis et al., 2017). The results from this and other studies indicate that only about a third of ADHD's heritability is due to the inheritance of many common gene variants, each having small effects (Faraone & Larsson, 2018). This is known as the *missing heritability* problem in that commonly occurring genetic variants explain only a fraction of heritability, not only in ADHD but all psychiatric disorders (Beauchaine, Gatzky-Kopp, & Gizer, 2017). Much of the missing heritability may not be due to as as-yet undiscovered common gene variants (Zuk, Hechtner, Sunyaev, & Lander, 2012). Some may be due to rare genetic variants or

[2] GWAS involves scanning an entire genome of many people to find genetic variants associated with a particular trait or disorder (Beauchaine, Gatzky-Kopp, & Gizer, 2017). The set of DNA sequences that constitutes the human genome consists of about 3 million base pairs and about 20,000 protein-coding genes counting just one chromosome from each pair of the 23 pairs of chromosomes (Knopik et al., 2017). The DNA (deoxyribonucleic acid) molecule consists of two strands that are held apart by pairs of four bases: adenine, thymine, guanine, and cytosine. The most widely studied type of genetic variation is a single nucleotide polymorphism, in which a single base pair at a defined location in the genome varies among individuals in the population (Gizer, Otto, & Ellingson, 2016). Gene variants occurring with a frequency of >1% in the general population are deemed *common*; gene variants occurring with a frequency of <1% are deemed *rare* (Gizer et al., 2016).

copy number variants (deletions or duplications of large genomic segments spanning a part of a gene or entire gene) undetected by GWAS (Faraone & Larsson, 2018). In such rare cases, a single genetic defect alone may cause ADHD (Faraone & Larsson, 2018). Also, a substantial portion of the unexplained heritable variation may be due to limitations in the ability GWAS to detect genetic variation that is caused by *nonadditivity,* i.e., it is not caused by the independent effects of genes that add up to influence a phenotypic characteristic (Knopik et al., 2017). This nonadditive variation can be caused by gene by gene interactions, gene-environment correlation, gene by environment interactions, and epigenetic effects (Knopik et al., 2017; Mayhew & Meyre, 2017; Nigg, 2017a).

Gene-by-gene interaction refers to the effect of two or more genes that is much larger than the simple increase in risk conferred by each gene. In behavioral genetics this is called *epistasis* (Knopik et al., 2017). For example, assume that there are two genes, each of which confers a 1% risk for ADHD. If a child were to inherit both genes, the risk for ADHD would be 2%, as the effect of each gene is added up. However, if there were *epistasis*, having both genes might result in an 10% increase because of their interaction (Barkley, 2017).

Gene-environment correlation refers to processes by which genes contribute to variations in environments that individuals experience and thereby contribute to variations in the trait influenced by the genes (Knopik et al., 2017). There are three types of gene-environment correlation. *Passive genotype-environment correlation* occurs when the child's behavior and the environment his or her parents provide are correlated because they have the same origins in the parents' genotype, as is the case for the 25% to 35% of children with ADHD who have at least one parent with ADHD. In this scenario, the parent's impulsivity and disorganization can make the challenging task of raising a child with ADHD become "exponentially harder and a sure-fire recipe for family chaos" (Hinshaw & Ellison, 2016, p. 35). This chaos can increase the severity of their child's ADHD symptoms and disruptive behavior (Hinshaw & Ellison, 2016; Johnston & Chronis-Tuscano, 2015). *Evocative genotype-environment correlation* occurs when children, on the basis of their genetic tendencies, evoke reactions from other people. For example, research has found that children with ADHD symptoms who were adopted provoked hostile parenting, which in turn increased the severity of their ADHD symptoms (Hinshaw & Ellison, 2016). *Active genotype-environment correlation* occurs when individuals select environments that are correlated with their genetic tendencies. The reader will recall the quote from Hallowell and Ratey (2005, p.25) that: *Many of us with ADHD crave high-stimulus situations.* Consequently, *a craving for high stimulation can get a person into trouble.*

Gene by environment interactions and epigenetic effects will be examined in the following section on environmental factors as they probably are the main mechanisms by which environmental risk factors increase risk for ADHD (Faraone et al., 2015; Nigg, 2018) and therefore merit a more expansive discussion.

Lastly, it should be noted that ADHD can be caused by genetic variants, called mutations, that are not inherited (Barkley, 2017). Mutations refer to mistakes made in copying the genes of a child that are not present in the genes inherited from the parent. They are termed new or *de novo* mutations because they do not affect the parent but occur because mistakes are made during the formation of parent's egg or sperm (Knopik et al., 2017). These new mutations can be inherited by the children's offspring. Because evolution has so finely tuned the genetic systems, any mistakes made in copying will generally have harmful effects (Knopik et al., 2017).

Environmental Factors

Although environmental factors such as severe traumatic brain injury may directly cause ADHD in some cases (Barkley, 2015e), gene-by-environment interaction and epigenetic processes are considered the main mechanisms by which environmental risk factors increase the risk for ADHD (Faraone et al., 2015; Nigg, 2018). These mechanisms will be discussed first, followed by a discussion of some well-established environmental factors

Gene by Environment Interaction

Gene by environment interaction (GxE) refers to situations in which environments moderate effects of genes on behavior (Beauchaine, Gatzke-Kopp, & Gizer, 2017). In this mechanism as previously discussed, ADHD is not conceptualized primarily as a condition caused by the inheritance of a certain number of genes. Rather, what is inherited are genes that confer a liability. This genetic liability is then thought to interact with certain environmental risks to trigger the disorder. For example, Barkley (2017) notes that a child's prenatal exposure to alcohol increases the risk for ADHD about 2.5 times the population risk. However, if the child has a genetic vulnerability to ADHD, the interaction of this vulnerability with prenatal alcohol exposure may increase the risk for ADHD 8 times that of the general population. This model therefore suggests that a given environmental risk will not affect all children. Some children may be "immune" to the effect (Nigg, 2017b, p. 416), but others with a genetic vulnerability to ADHD would develop the disorder in the presence of the environmental risk factor. Nigg (2018, p. E1) suggests that "While the magnitude of gene-by-environment effects in ADHD remains unclear, it is possible, perhaps even likely, that genotype (liability)-environment (modulation) interplay is fundamental." Accordingly, it is now recognized that genetic liabilities and environment risks almost never operate as independent causes but interact in complex ways to produce various mental disorders (Beauchaine, Gatzke-Kopp, & Gizer, 2017).

Epigenetics

Epigenetics, meaning "over the genome," refers to biochemical mechanisms whereby environmental factors induce changes in gene expression (Bhat, Joober, & Sengupta, 2017). The environmental factors include a range of biological and psychological events which cause the body to form a chemical marker that attaches to the DNA molecule, thereby altering gene expression (Beauchaine et al., 2017b; Nigg, 2017b). As these chemical markers sit "over" the DNA, they do not alter its sequence. The changes tend to be stable but can be erased by subsequent environmental events. There is also some evidence for the multigenerational transmission (i.e., inheritance) of these changes (Nigg, 2018). Some however have expressed concern that "epigenetic has been wildly oversold" (Moffitt & Beckley, 2015, p.124). Because studies are just beginning to emerge that have found evidence for this mechanism, we do not yet know how much of ADHD heritability is epigenetic rather than genetic (Nigg, 2017b, 2018).

Environmental Risk Factors

Identifying environmental risk factors for ADHD that are causal can be very challenging methodologically because the studies are exclusively based upon observational designs in which an association/correlation is observed between a putative environmental risk factor and ADHD. The reason for the exclusive use of observational studies to examine environmental risk factors is that it is ethically impermissible to expose an individual to a risk factor to study its effects on ADHD. For example, suppose one wanted to examine whether or not prenatal exposure to maternal smoking caused ADHD. It is obviously unethical to experimentally *manipulate* this variable by randomly assigning some pregnant women to smoke and others to not smoke. Therefore, since randomly controlled trials (RCT)[3], the gold standard with respect to causal inference (Jaffee, Strait, & Odgers, 2012; Rutter & Thapar, 2016) for smoking and virtually any other potential risk factor for ADHD cannot be conducted, causal inference can only be determined by *observing*, not *manipulating* the association of a risk factor and ADHD. This limitation in observational studies, which is not unique to ADHD but characterizes much of the research on psychopathology (Jaffee et al., 2012), inevitably involves several potential problems in trying to determine causation. Two problems are most relevant for interpreting an association between an alleged environmental risk factor and ADHD as a cause-effect association (Jaffee et al., 2012; Rutter & Thapar, 2016).

The first problem is the possibility of *reverse causation* (Jaffee et al., 2012; Rutter & Thapar, 2016). For example, the well documented association between excessive video game playing and ADHD could be explained in two ways. Video game playing could cause ADHD-like inattentive symptoms. Or, ADHD could cause individuals to be more likely to engage in these activities than those without ADHD because of the highly stimulating/rewarding nature of the game stimuli (Hinshaw & Ellison, 2016). There is a robust consensus that although excessive video gaming may exacerbate ADHD symptoms, it is the ADHD = excessive video gaming that drives the association (Barkley, 2015e; Hinshaw & Ellison, 2016; Nigg, 2017b). As Nigg (2017b, p. 118) has concluded, "…too much media does weaken attention and add to ADHD, but only slightly."

---

[3] In an RCT experimental design there are at least two conditions to which participants are randomly assigned using, for example, a coin toss. Ideally, neither the participants nor the experimenter(s) know which condition each group has been assigned to (i.e., they are *blinded*). For example, children would be randomly assigned to a diet which includes a food additive which is hypothesized to cause ADHD and an additive that is known not to cause ADHD with both the child (and parent) and experimenter blinded. If ADHD occurs, then the cause would have to be the food additive since by the logic of randomization all other unmeasured factors are randomized out (i.e., cancel one another out) thereby making the groups equal except for the experimental manipulation (i.e., the food additive). Therefore, if the two groups differ in outcome in the hypothesized direction (ADHD) and the only difference between the groups is the experimentally induced difference (food additive), then the different outcome must be *caused* by the induced difference. They did not simply occur together.

The second problem, which is the central problem, is the possibility that some unknown third variable may account for the association (Moffitt, 2005). This variable is called a *confounder*, i.e., another variable associated with the putative risk variable that is the real cause of the outcome. For example, in the numerous studies which have found that children exposed to toxic levels of lead are at increased risk for ADHD, these children may also have worse diets. Therefore, maybe it is the poor diet that that causes the ADHD and not the lead.

The third variable may be heritable (Moffitt, 2005; Rutter & Thapar, 2016). For example, in the ADHD literature there is wide acceptance that prenatal exposure to maternal smoking may play a causal role in ADHD because of the consistency of findings across numerous studies that have used state of the art statistical analyses to control for various confounders (Schechter & Kollins, 2017). However, mothers who smoke during pregnancy may differ in many respects from those who do not smoke during pregnancy that could not be statistically controlled for in such studies such as having ADHD risk-genes which their offspring inherit. This possibility was investigated in studies using three different types of designs to separate confounding possibly due to genetic factors from the effects of prenatal exposure to maternal smoking. In the first type of design, studies examined the rates of ADHD among siblings who either were or were not exposed prenatally to maternal smoking (Gutavson et al., 2017; Obel et al., 2016; Skoglund et al., 2014). All studies found an elevated risk for ADHD, but it was the same level of risk for siblings not exposed prenatally to maternal smoking suggesting that the association was due to some unmeasured confounder, e.g., genetic inheritance. In a second type of design, a study by Gutavson and colleagues (2017) used a negative control approach which compares the association of interest with another association that is not expected to be causal. The study found that maternal smoking was not more strongly associated with offspring ADHD than was paternal smoking during maternal pregnancy, or grandmother's smoking when she was pregnant with mother, or maternal smoking during previous pregnancies. Therefore the results suggest that the association between maternal smoking during pregnancy and offspring ADHD is not causal but due to some unmeasured confounding, e..g., genetic inheritance. In a third type of design, Thapar and colleagues (2009) compared offspring conceived through in vitro fertilization by using eggs from the mother or from genetically unrelated women. The results indicated that the magnitude of association between maternal smoking during pregnancy was significantly higher in the genetically related mother-offspring pairs than in the unrelated pairs. This once again suggests that the relationship between maternal smoking during pregnancy and offspring ADHD reflects genetic confounding. Therefore, as Rutter and Thapar (2016, p. 149) concluded in the their review of this literature, "prenatal exposure to maternal smoking does not have a causal effect in leading to ADHD."

In conclusion, the studies that have proposed various environmental causal risk factors for ADHD are on more tenuous evidentiary footing than those that have established genetic causes for ADHD. Nevertheless, as Jaffee and colleagues (2012) have demonstrated with regard to environmental risk factors and antisocial behavior, there can be a convergence of evidence from studies using sophisticated design methods that can determine whether risk factors that have repeatedly been identified across numerous observational studies are likely to play a causal role.

Only a few of the environmental risk factors for ADHD will now be examined as the purpose of the discussion is to illustrate how environment can influence the development of ADHD rather than to provide a comprehensive review. The reader who may be interested in more extensive coverage should consult Barkley (2015e) and Nigg (2017a).

Traumatic Brain Injury

Some cases of ADHD can be directly acquired as a consequence of exposure to various biohazards (Barkley, 2015e). Perhaps the best example of such a biohazard is a severe traumatic brain injury. This is because the effects on the brain are so devastating that it will adversely affect all individuals who sustain such a trauma. It does not require an interaction with a genetic vulnerability to exert its harmful effects (Barkley, 2015e). One of those effects can be ADHD. Other more subtle forms of brain injury such as those caused by premature birth or exposure to certain environmental chemicals, as will subsequently be discussed, are more likely to exert their impact in interaction with a genetic liability to ADHD (Nigg, 2017b).

Traumatic brain injuries (TBIs) are a major cause of death and disability, with a world-wide annual incidence ~10 million people (Blennow et al., 2016). They include two major types of injuries. In the first type an object such as bullet *penetrates* the skull and directly damages the brain in a specific location. In the second type, close-*headed* injuries, which can be caused by falls or car accidents, the skull remains intact. This type of injury, which is by far the most common, causes damage indirectly by shaking[4] the brain within the skull, resulting in multifocal injuries. Other mechanisms of injury include intracerebral hematomas (accumulation of blood within the brain), hypoxia (oxygen deprivation), edema (collection of watery fluid) and intracranial pressure (McAllister, 2008). TBIs can be categorized into mild, moderate, and severe based upon criteria such as duration of loss of consciousness (if any), presence of amnesia, neurological symptoms, and the results of brain imaging techniques (Blennow et al., 2016).

Beginning with the classic case of Phineas Gage in 1848 (Damasio, 1994), research has shown that TBI's affecting the brain's frontal lobes can result in symptoms similar to ADHD (Arciniegas & Wortzel, 2014; Yeates, 2010). Hence it is not surprising that a number of studies that have specifically assessed for ADHD caused by TBI in childhood have found that the symptoms and accompanying impairments are so severe that they qualify for a DSM diagnosis of ADHD (Gerring & Vasa, 2016; Max, 2014). Such diagnoses are designated secondary ADHD (SADHD) to distinguish it from neurodevelopmental ADHD. Eme (2015) reviewed this literature, comprising 9 different studies and concluded that the rate of SADHD was approximately 25% for those with severe TBIs. The majority of juveniles were assessed for SADHD at least two years after the TBI. The problem of confounders in all the studies was addressed in two ways. First, pre-injury ADHD cases, which can occur in approximately 20% to 30% of juvenile TBI cases, were excluded (Eme, 2015). Second, several studies controlled for the possible confounder of the trauma of sustaining any kind of physical injury causing SADHD by employing a control group of children who had sustained an orthopedic injury (OI). In such instances, the rate of ADHD in the OI group was no greater than would be expected from the population prevalence of ADHD (Eme, 2015). Most recently, Narad and colleagues (2018) provided impressive support for TBI as a cause of SADHD. They examined the development of SADHD 5 to 10 years after 187 children had sustained a TBI between 3-7 years of age. An astounding 62% of children with a severe TBI developed SADHD, most within 18 months of sustaining the TBI. This rate was 4 times higher than the OI group.

---

[4] More precisely, this "shaking" refers to the rapid acceleration and/or deceleration of the brain within the skull which generates shearing and strain forces that stretch and damage the brain's axons. An axon is the part of a neuron that transfers a nerve impulse from the nerve cell body to another nerve cell. This type of injury, termed diffuse axonal injury, can be thought of as pervasively damaging the brain's wiring.

Lastly, it should be noted that to the author's knowledge no study assessing for a formal DSM diagnosis of ADHD following adult TBI has yet been conducted. However, it is reasonable to assume that the risk for SADHD would presumably also apply to adults since symptoms of inattentiveness and impulsivity are among the most prominent symptoms following a TBI for both children and adults (Anderson & Yeates, 2014; McAllister, 2008).

Pregnancy and Birth Complications

For more than 50 years studies have examined the relationship between ADHD and numerous pregnancy and birth complications such as low birth weight, prematurity, preeclampsia, induced labor, asphyxia and many others (Barkley, 2015e; Sciberras, Mulrany, Silva, & Cognill, 2017). Establishing a truly causal relationship between these risk factors and ADHD is particularly challenging because of the great difficulty in eliminating potential confounders such as genetic inheritance, gestational age, inadequate prenatal nutrition, maternal smoking, drug use, etc. (Momany, Kamracht, & Nikolas, 2017). Because of this difficulty, the only complication with robust empirical support is low birth weight (Franz et al., 2018; Momany et al., 2017, Nigg & Song, 2018). A meta-analysis of 88 studies (N=4,645,482) showed that birth weight has a small, but significant linkage to ADHD symptoms (Momany et al., 2017). Children born at lower birth weights manifested greater symptoms of ADHD (r=-0.15). This linkage probably increases as birth weight becomes lower (Momany et al., 2017). The threshold for low birth weight is being born at less than 5lbs. 8oz, with very low birth weight being less than 3lbs. 4oz. For example, a meta-analysis of 12 studies (N=1787) by Franz and colleagues (2018) found that very low birth weight was associated with a striking increased risk for ADHD ~300%. Thus, low birth weight may be the single strongest known environmental risk factor for ADHD (Nigg & Song, 2018). One possible causal pathway linking low weight to ADHD is via an insufficient supply of blood and oxygen to the brain in utero (Momany et al., 2017).

Environmental Toxins

Of the multitude of environmental toxins and chemicals that have been linked to ADHD, the evidence for exposure to lead is the most convincing (Barkley, 2015e; Nigg, 2017b). This exposure can come from numerous sources such as: leaching of water pipes, air pollution, chipping paint, and contaminated soil where lead products were previously used (Nigg, 2017b). However, as previously discussed, since for ethical reasons children cannot be randomly assigned to groups that either are exposed to lead or not, studies must rely on correlational designs with the inevitable problem of third variable confounds. For example, it may be that children with exposure to toxic levels of lead also have worse diets than children who are not so exposed. Therefore, maybe it is the poor diet that that causes the ADHD and not the lead. However, for lead these methodological challenges were overcome to the extent that is possible to so in a recent study. Drawing upon nature's random assignment of genes that affect how efficiently the body metabolizes lead, a study was able to identify two groups of children who were either of high or low efficiency in metabolizing lead (Nigg, 2017b; Nigg, Elmore, Natarajan, Friderici, & Nicholas, 2016.) Consistent with the proposition that lead plays a causal role in some cases of ADHD, children with the low efficiency metabolism had higher levels of hyperactive-impulsive symptoms than children with the high efficiency metabolism. The study's authors theorized that the increased levels of lead in the children with the low efficiency metabolism resulted in an epigenetic modification of a brain neural circuit related to hyperactivity-impulsivity. Although the size of the blood level interaction with the lead metabolizing genes on the expression of hyperactive-impulsive symptoms was modest, it provided an example of a GxE with possible epigenetic effects in the development of ADHD. In short, the study validated the hypothesis that there can be an interaction between a genetic vulnerability and an environmental risk factor that has a causal effect on some cases of ADHD. The evidence for interactions between other specific genes and other environmental toxins is less robust as none of them to the author's knowledge has been studied using the design that was involved in the lead study.

Psychosocial Factors
Adversity, Stress, Trauma

Nigg (2017b) notes that until recently adversity, stress, and trauma have been something of "blind spot" (p. 162) in the study of ADHD. Current reviews of the relationship between these factors and ADHD have yielded the following conclusions (Barkley, 2015e; Hinshaw, 2018; Musser, Peris, Karalunas, Dieckman, & Nigg, 2016; Nigg, 2017b). First, these factors as well as others such as maladaptive parenting, play a causal role in increasing the likelihood that children with ADHD will develop other disorders, including particular antisocial disorders, as will be discussed in a subsequent chapter. Second, it is likely that stress induced by high levels of parental criticism can contribute to the persistence of ADHD. Third, because of their behavioral and emotional impulsivity, children with ADHD are more likely than children without ADHD to be exposed to and to have a worse reaction to adversity, stress, and trauma. For example, a meta-analysis of 28 studies of ADHD and trauma found that children with ADHD are 60% more likely to have a serious adverse experience as a consequence of ADHD (Spencer et al., 2016). Fourth, in some rare cases, there may be a predominantly psychosocial pathway to ADHD. The most compelling evidence comes from studies of children raised in institutional settings and then placed in adoptive or foster families (Kennedy et al., 2016). Children exposed to institutional care often suffer from profound neglect which may include "minimum physical resources, unfavorable and unstable staffing patterns, and socially, emotionally inadequate caregiver- child interactions" (van Ijzendoorn et al., 2011, p. 8) resulting in myriad of adverse developmental outcomes. One of those outcomes is elevated levels of inattention and hyperactivity/impulsivity (Kennedy et al., 2016). Perhaps the most compelling evidence of this outcome comes from the English and Romanian Adoptees (ERA) study (Kennedy et al., 2016; Nigg, 2017b). The study involved a follow-up into young adulthood (ages 22-25 years) of 165 children who lived for up to 3 ½ years in extreme deprivation in institutions in Romania and who were subsequently adopted by families living in the United Kingdom. These individuals upon follow-up were over seven (29.3%) times more likely to meet criteria for ADHD (mostly the predominantly inattentive presentation) than those who had experienced low levels of deprivation (other adoptees in the United Kingdom). Crucially, it is also important to note that the increased risk for ADHD was found despite the individuals having spent the vast majority of their lives (i.e., from 3 ½ years or earlier) in loving, supportive, and well-resourced families. However, their presentation of ADHD was not typical in that it occurred with high levels of autism spectrum disorder, disinhibited social engagement, and callous-unemotional traits.[5] Since such cases are very rare as a cause of ADHD, the primary value of the study is to confirm the principle that ADHD, despite its atypical form, can apparently be caused by severe early adversity (Nigg, 2017b). It is not known how well the findings of the ERA and other studies of severe early

---

[5] Such traits include a lack of guilt and remorse, a lack of concern for the feelings of others, and shallow or superficial emotions (Frick, Ray, Thornton, & Kahn, 2014).

deprivation extend to the lesser levels of and far more common kinds of stress, adversity and trauma that children may encounter (Nigg, 2017b). Fifth, sufficient stress, adversity and trauma can increase the risk of "ADHD-like" symptoms in children (Nigg, 2017b, p. 167). However, as Nigg (2017b) cautions, the resulting problems with self-regulation need to be understood as something other than ADHD and require a different therapeutic approach. Nevertheless, it is possible that stress, adversity, and trauma in the context of genetic liability and other aspects of the early environment can increase risk for ADHD through producing epigenetic changes in the genome (Nigg, 2017b).

In conclusion, except in the case of extreme deprivation, there is no evidence that psychosocial factors alone (e.g., poor parenting), however much they may contribute to the development of other problems in individuals with ADHD or the persistence of ADHD, can directly cause ADHD (Barkley, 2015e; Hinshaw & Ellison, 2016). There remains, however, the newly emerging possibility that psychosocial risk factors such as adversity, stress, and trauma can interact with genetic vulnerabilities through epigenetic mechanisms to increase risk for ADHD (Nigg, 2017b).

Brain Mechanisms of ADHD

The effects of the complex interplay between genetic liability and environmental risk factors are mediated through alterations of brain maturation, structure, function and neural transmission (Barkley, 2015e; Brown, 2017; Gallo & Posner, 2016; Nigg, 2017a). These alterations in turn adversely affect cognitive and neuropsychological functioning regulated by various brain neural circuits.

Brain Maturation

Shaw and colleagues (2007, 2012, 2013) have conducted three studies using magnetic resonance imaging (MRI) to investigate brain maturation in children with ADHD compared to typically developing children. The MRI utilizes the different magnetic properties of brain tissue to study the structure of the brain. In the first study, the brains of 223 children diagnosed with ADHD and 233 normally developing subjects were scanned to estimate cortical thickness as they were growing up. The study found that there was a marked delay in the brains of children with ADHD in attaining peak cortical thickness throughout most of the brain. The most prominent delay (3-years) was in the prefrontal cortex which is the most important brain structure for regulation of attention, behavior, and emotion. A second imaging study of the same subjects also found a delay in the maturation of cortical surface area in children with ADHD compared to typically developing children that mirrored the delayed maturation of cortical thickness that was found in the prior study. As with the first study, the authors were able to determine that the delayed maturation was unlikely to be attributable to the effects of treatment with stimulant medication. A third study involved a sample of 92 individuals who had been diagnosed with ADHD in childhood and had an MRI prior to age 17 and again in young adulthood (average age of 24). The sample was divided into those who still had ADHD (40%) and those whose ADHD had remitted (60%). The brain images from both groups were then compared to the brain images from a control group of 184 typically developing young adults. The MRI found that in those adults whose ADHD had remitted the cortex had thickened just as it had in a typically developing group indicating that their brain development had caught up. There was no such "catch-up" in the group whose ADHD had persisted (primarily inattentive symptoms). The extent to which "catch-up" this takes place is an open question (Hinshaw & Ellison, 2016) with most individuals with ADHD not showing a complete development "catch-up" (Faraone et al., 2015). More recently, a study using MRI scans from 23 research centers and involving over 1,700 individuals with ADHD and more than 1500 without ADHD (ranging in age from 4-63) also found that those with ADHD had delayed maturation in a variety of subcortical structures (Hoogman et al., 2017).

Lastly, it is important to reiterate that the studies also showed that it was highly unlikely that the previous use of stimulant medication for ADHD caused the brain immaturity. If anything, some research has shown that use of stimulant medication is associated with more normal brain development (Lugo-Candelas & Posner, 2017; Shaw et al., 2012, 2013).

Brain Structure

A range of structural brain alterations have been found in individuals with ADHD (Faraone et al., 2015). For example, several studies have found that on average children with ADHD have a 5% reduction in overall brain volume and a 12% reduction in volume of key frontal and subcortical structures, including the cerebellum (Faraone et al., 2015; Nigg, 2017a). The findings on the prefrontal cortex (PFC) (the region behind the forehead) are perhaps the most significant since it is the most involved in self-regulation with Barkley (2015e) referring to it as the "executive brain" (p. 364). More recently these findings have also been extended to preschool children. The first comprehensive examination of cortical volume of preschool children ages 4-5 years with ADHD (52 with ADHD, unmedicated, and 38 controls) found widespread cortical reductions in those with ADHD (Jacobson et al., 2018). Moreover, the reductions showing greatest effect size were noted in regions important for functions such as inhibitory control and planning.

Brain Functioning

Brain activity can be measured using functional magnetic resonance imaging (fMRI). FMRI is sensitive to oxygenation of the blood. It measures brain function based on the premise that active cells consume oxygen leading to increased blood flow. Comparisons are then made between individuals with and without ADHD to assess brain activity while performing a certain task. For example, a commonly used task is a stop-signal task for measuring impulsivity. In this task, the participant must respond to an arrow stimulus by selecting one of two options, depending on the direction in which the arrow points. If an audio tone is present, the subject must withhold the impulse to make a response. Numerous research studies using such tasks have found lower activation indicative of abnormal functioning in several brain neural circuits in those with ADHD compared to those without ADHD (Faraone et al., 2015; Nigg, 2017a). In addition to abnormal functioning within brain circuits, other studies using another neuroimaging technique, diffusion tensor imaging, have investigated the connections within and between brain circuits. This method traces the directional flow/diffusion of water molecules to assess the integrity of axonal connections (white matter). An axon is the long slender projection of neuron that uses electrical impulses and chemical signals to transmit information between the brain's neurons. The axon has a fatty (white) covering that forms a protective sheath around nerve fibers and dramatically speeds the transmission of nerve signals. In short, axons can be thought of as the neural wiring among various brain regions. Again, several studies of children, adolescents, and adults with ADHD have found widespread abnormalities in this wiring (Barkley, 2015e; Nigg, 2017a; Posner, Park, & Wang, 2014; Yoncheva et al., 2016).

Neural Transmission

Neurons communicate with one another through various chemical messengers called neurotransmitters. A deficiency in a number of different neurotransmitters has been implicated in the etiology of ADHD (Barkley, 2015a). This discussion will focus on dopamine (DA) as it is the neurotransmitter that has been most extensively investigated (Barkley, 2015e; Levy, 2007). It is also the neurotransmitter that is most relevant to understanding how ADHD increases risk for criminal behavior, as will subsequently be discussed. The most impressive evidence connecting a DA deficiency to the etiology of ADHD comes from hundreds of studies that have demonstrated that stimulant medications significantly improve cognitive and behavioral functioning at least in the short-term (e.g., over several weeks or months) for most children and adults with ADHD by increasing the level of DA (Barkley, 2015e; Brown, 2017; Connor, 2015; Hinshaw & Ellison, 2016). Thus, by inference, a DA deficiency must be involved in ADHD. The deficiency in DA can be caused by the brain making too little of it, having fewer receptors on a neuron to receive it, or using it less efficiently (Hinshaw & Ellison, 2016). In addition to this indirect evidence, there is some evidence from studies using direct measures of the availability of DA that have also found a DA deficiency (Barkley, 2015e).

Neural Networks Implicated in ADHD

Although it is not yet possible to distill the mosaic of the various studies into a single comprehensive neurobiological theory of ADHD, the preceding studies on brain maturation, structure, function, and neural transmission in ADHD have implicated several large-scale networks[6] in ADHD (Faraone et al., 2015), with the evidence being strongest for five networks important for self-regulation. The networks subserve sustained attention, alertness, motivation, inhibitory control, and emotional regulation (Castellanos & Aoki, 2016; Gallo & Posner, 2016; Rubia, 2018).[7] Since the networks may vary in their involvement in ADHD, this may explain some of the heterogeneity in how ADHD presents across individuals (Barkley, 2015e). (See Figure 2-1)

---

[6] A neural network is a system of discreet brain regions with connections between them (Uddin & Karlsgodt, 2018).

[7] There is also consistent evidence for a dysfunctional corticocerebellar network which is involved in complex motor activity and temporal processing (Faraone et al., 2015; Nigg, 2017a). This network will not be discussed since motor activity is not relevant to self-regulation and the linkage between deficits in temporal processing such as poor time estimation and self-regulation requires more research (Nigg, 2017a).

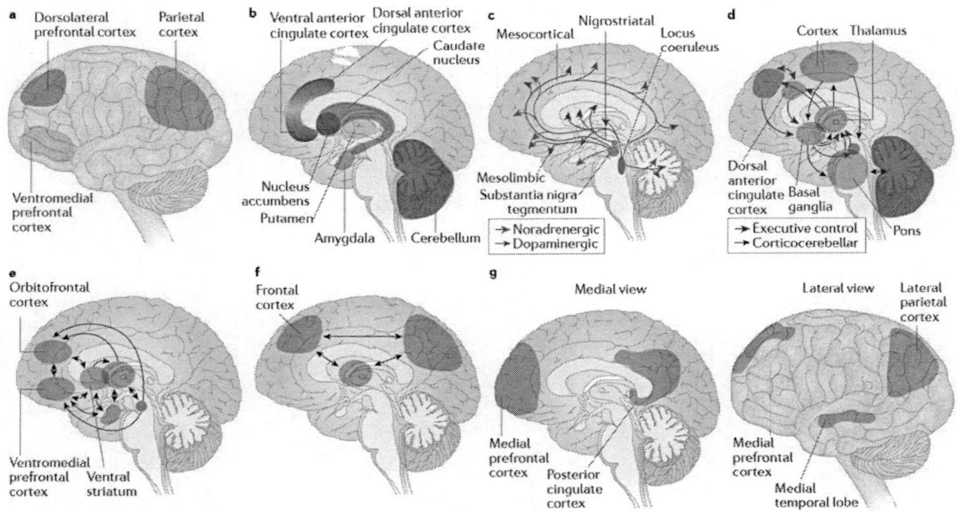

a|Cortical regions. **b**|Subcortical . **c**|Dopamine system. **d**|Executive control networks.

e|Reward network. **f**| Attention network. **g**|DMN network (medial and lateral views).

Adapted with copywrite permission from Springer Nature

Figure 2-1

There is a cingulo-opercular network (Figure 1f) that regulates sustained attention by facilitating the maintenance of effort on a task and suppressing competing information (Nigg, 2016). This network involves the dorsal anterior cingulate/medial superior frontal cortex and bilateral anterior insula/frontal operculum (Neta, Nelson, & Petersen, 2017). As tasks become more complex and of longer duration other attention networks may also become involved (Nigg, 2016).

The second network is the brain's default mode network (DMN) or "resting" brain (Hinshaw & Ellison, 2016; Posner, Park, & Wang, 2014) [Figure 1g]. The DMN is an interconnected network of brain regions demonstrating high neural activity when individuals are at wakeful rest or engaged in internal tasks such as daydreaming (Posner et al., 2014; Rubia, 2018). When individuals transition from internally-focused to external goal directed tasks, the DMN becomes deactivated. However, in ADHD this "resting state" brain activity does not deactivate. This results in daydreaming, mind-wandering affecting attention and thus task performance.

A third network, the mesolimbic dopamine (DA) network (Figure 1c), plays a crucial role in reinforcement and sustaining motivation (Volkow, Wise, & Baler, 2017). It will receive the lion's share of the ink because of its importance in understanding the neurobiological basis for behavioral impulsivity. DA is the neurotransmitter that is implicated in the neural processing of reward-related stimuli such as food, sex, including those associated with drugs of abuse (Volkow, 2015; Zisner & Beauchaine, 2016a). Rewards defined scientifically act as positive reinforcers/ motivators to induce learning, elicit movements towards a desired object, and elicit emotions such as pleasure and desire (Schultz, 2016). DA projections are divided into four primary neural systems, two of which are relevant to behavioral impulsivity: the mesolimbic and mesocortical (Beauchaine et al., 2017; Zisner & Beauchaine, 2016a) Several current comprehensive reviews concur in implicating impairments in both neural circuits and their interconnections to one another as well as other brain regions as the central neurobiological mechanisms in generating and controlling impulsivity (Beauchaine et al., 2017; Dalley & Robbins, 2017; Nigg, 2016; Ryan & Sequin, 2016). The mesolimbic dopamine circuit is most involved in impulse generation (Nigg, 2016). The subcortical mesolimbic DA network comprises DA neurons in the ventral tegmental area that project predominantly to the ventral striatum, including the nucleus accumbens and the ventral regions of the caudate nucleus and putamen. (Beauchaine et al., 2017; Zisner & Beauchaine, 2016). Subsequently, extensive neuroimaging research has found reduced mesolimbic activity during the anticipation of reward in individuals with ADHD (Beauchaine et al., 2017; Zisner & Beauchaine, 2016). This hypofunctioning of the mesolimbic circuit results in an undersensitivity to reinforcing stimuli which is hypothesized to trigger impulsivity in two major ways (Beauchaine et al., 2017; Zisner & Beauchaine, 2016a). First, undersensitivity leads to temporal discounting of reward in that individuals with ADHD find the experience in delay of reinforcement so aversive that they tend to impulsively choose immediate rewards even when an alternative option would result in larger reward after a longer delay. Second, undersensitivity leads to excessive, impulsive reward seeking as individuals with ADHD "experience relatively low hedonic value from pleasurable stimuli and therefore seek more frequent extreme incentives to derive hedonic payoff" (Zisner & Beauchaine, 2016b, p. 188) In short, undersensitivity to stimuli that most individuals would find reinforcing results in individuals with ADHD having chronic feelings of anhedonia which they find aversive. To alleviate such feelings, they tend to impulsively seek immediate and frequent reinforcement/gratification.

A fourth network, the mesocortical DA network (Figure 1c), plays a key role in inhibiting impulsive behavior. It involves neural projections from the ventral tegmental area to cerebral cortex, and the PFC and the anterior cingulate cortex (Ryan & Sequin, 2016). The PFC has four functional subdivisions: the dorsolateral, dorsomedial, ventromedial, and orbital prefrontal regions (Beauchaine et al., 2017; Carlen, 2017 Nigg, 2016; Petrovic & Castellanos, 2016). Each of these substructures is hypothesized to be somewhat differentially involved in impulse control (Gallo & Posner, 2016; Castellanos-Ryan & Sequin, 2016). A breakdown in optimal function and communication between the PFC and the midbrain region can result in failures to contain, inhibit, interrupt impulsive behavior (Castellanos-Ryan & Seguin, 2016).

The fifth network involves deficient regulation of emotional impulsivity (Figures 1d,e). As in the mesocortical DA network, the PFC plays a critical role in emotion regulation with different PFC regions differentially involved in different aspects of regulation (Dixon, Todd, Thiruchselvam, & Christoff, 2017). The most critical region is the orbitofrontal cortex with its two major functional regions (the lateral orbital frontal cortex and the medial orbital frontal cortex). This region along with the rostral anterior cingulate cortex and their respective connections to the subcortical areas of ventral striatum and the amygdala constitute the corticolimbic circuit (Dixon et al., 2017; MacDonald, Goines, Novacek, & Walker, 2016; Petrovic and Castellanos, 2016).

Conclusion

Copious evidence indicates that ADHD is a disorder involving some form of disruption of brain development. This evidence provides perhaps the most cogent validation of ADHD as a real disorder and not simply "problems in fidgeting and distractibility in middle-class, elementary school-aged boys who are parented too permissively and who contend with stifling classrooms" (Hinshaw, 2018, p. 2). Hence, the biological basis of its etiology has been discussed rather extensively to counter this all too common stereotypic presentation. Psychosocial factors, however much they may contribute to the development of other problems in individuals with ADHD or the persistence of ADHD, cannot directly cause ADHD except perhaps in cases of extraordinarily severe deprivation. There is also the possibility that psychosocial risk factors such as adversity, stress, and trauma can interact with genetic vulnerabilities through epigenetic mechanisms to increase risk for ADHD. Although the brain differences between groups of individuals with and without ADHD have been robustly documented in numerous studies, there is as yet no neurobiological marker to diagnose ADHD in individual cases (Thapar & Cooper, 2016), nor is there any such marker for other psychiatric disorders (Hinshaw & Scheffler, 2016). Recent findings using pattern recognition analyses of functioning neuroimaging data to diagnose ADHD are at the "promising" stage, requiring much more research (Rubia, 2018).

CHAPTER THREE

DEVELOPMENTAL OUTCOMES

The developmental outcomes of ADHD will be considered in terms of persistence into adulthood and impairments in important areas of life. The developmental outcome of criminality will be addressed in the following chapter.

Persistence of ADHD

The extent of the persistence of ADHD into adolescence and adulthood is the potential developmental outcome most relevant to the criminal justice system. For if childhood ADHD does not persist to any significant extent into the subsequent developmental periods, then whatever its role may have been in triggering a development cascade that led to criminal behavior, its relevance as an important current risk factor for maintaining criminal behavior is nil. Indeed, as recently as a couple of decades ago, most experts thought that ADHD symptoms vanished by adulthood (Hinshaw, 2018). We know now from the findings of several long term longitudinal studies that this is wrong[1] (Caye et al., 2016; Hechtman, 2017; Owens et al., 2015). The major findings from these studies will now be reviewed. A related issue—whether there is adult-onset ADHD—will also be considered.

Rate of Persistence

Longitudinal studies have clearly demonstrated that there is a high rate of persistence of ADHD from childhood to adolescence (50-80%) and into adulthood (35-65%) [Owens et al., 2015]. The rather wide range in persistence is not solely due to the difference in samples but also to the different ways in which ADHD has been assessed (Sibley et al., 2017). As previously discussed, methods that use DSM-5 criteria, obtain information

---

[1] A longitudinal study is an observational research method in which data is gathered for the same subjects repeatedly over a period of time.

from collateral informants, and use norm-referenced criteria will yield more accurate, higher rates of persistence (Sibley et al., 2017). Thus, the true rate of persistent ADHD symptoms most likely resides in the upper range of the previously cited estimates of 50%-80% from childhood to adolescence and 35%-65% into adulthood. For example, the most recent follow-up of the MTA study which employed these methods reported a 60% rate of symptom persistence into young adulthood (Sibley et al., 2017). This rate is probably even higher since, as previously discussed, the decline in symptoms may be illusory as the DSM-5 list of symptoms is developmentally insensitive to manifestations of ADHD at older ages.

In determing the persistence of ADHD, a distinction must be made between ADHD symptoms and ADHD-related impairments. For example, in MTA study Sibley and colleagues (2017) reported that although 60% of the ADHD group demonstrated symptom persistence when followed-up to a mean age of 25, only 41% of the group met both symptom and impairment criteria for ADHD. The discrepancy between the rate of symptom persistence and symptom/impairment was attributed to the likelihood that the ADHD symptoms were well-managed and therefore no longer impairing. However, the decline in impairment might be somewhat deceptive for two reasons. First, as Faraone and colleagues (2015) have contended, if symptomatic/unimpaired individuals went to such great lengths to manage their symptoms that these exertions caused significant distress, or perhaps prevented the individuals from engaging in other activities, then impairment is present. Second, the absence of impairment may also be misleading because, as previously discussed, ADHD is not a static condition. Across situations and over the course of a lifetime symptoms can be well-managed in some circumstances and not in others, with resulting fluctuations in impairment (Brown, 2017). A prime example of such fluctuation cited by Brown (2017) and evidenced in two of the author's cases involves a change in a work setting. Two adults with ADHD, one male and one female who were highly successful in sales became markedly dysfunctional when the change in their job situation required a much higher level of organizational skills than previously required. In the case of the male, he was promoted to a desk job. In the case of the female, she lost a long time assistant who was in charge of scheduling. He was fired from his job and her success plummeted. This raises the question as to whether or not a person whose ADHD is well-managed either because of strenuous exertions, favorable situations, or effective treatment should continue to be diagnosed with the disorder. Rutter (2011), for one, would answer yes. He makes an argument, easily applied to ADHD, that "…it would be absurd not to diagnose diabetes that is well controlled by treatment, just because there was not impairment at the moment. The same would apply to schizophrenia that is well controlled by appropriate medication" (Rutter, 2011, p. 656).

In conclusion, while ADHD was once thought to be limited to childhood, evidence from numerous longitudinal studies clearly shows that this is not the case. A substantial majority of individuals with childhood ADHD continue to have the disorder into adulthood. This conclusion however needs to be tempered by a limitation in most of these studies. Because the studies involved participants drawn from clinics who tend to have a more severe form of ADHD than those in the community (Hechtman, 2017), it is not known to what extent the rates of persistence and impairment generalize to children who are not clinic-referred. Most probably the rate of persistence in community cases of ADHD is less than that of clinic cases since severity of ADHD and co-occurring conduct problems which predict persistence are more characteristic of clinic cases (Hechtman, 2017). Lastly, considering all the research, a reasonable ballpark estimate of the persistence of childhood ADHD into adulthood has been provided by Lee, Sibley, and Epstein (2016). They estimate that adult outcomes of individuals with childhood ADHD roughly fall into three equivalently sized groups: positively adjusted, moderately impaired, and severely impaired

Adult-Onset ADHD?

Having established the reality of adult ADHD due to the persistence of child-onset ADHD, a very recent issue is whether there also are cases of adult-onset ADHD. Recent birth cohort studies[2] have reported a 2.5% to 10.7% prevalence for cases of ADHD that first occur in adolescence or adulthood, thereby contradicting the longstanding consensus that ADHD is a disorder that only first appears in childhood (i.e., before age 12 in DSM-5) [Caye et al., 2016; Moffitt et al., 2015; Sibley et al., 2018]. However, critics have suggested that these cases may represent individuals whose symptoms were either undetected or sub-threshold and only became evident when environmental demands or risk factors increased later in life (Asherson et al., 2016; Faraone & Biederman, 2016). Also, these cases may represent false positives due to sole reliance on screening instruments or failure to consider other mental disorders as the source of the symptoms

[2] A birth cohort study is a type of longitudinal study which follows the lives of a group of people all born at the same time and gathers information on the group at various points over the course of the study.

(Sibley et al., 2018). Sibley and colleagues (2018) addressed the limitations in the birth cohort studies using subjects from the MTA study. This study was carefully designed to assess ADHD symptoms over time using comprehensive psychiatric evaluations with multi-informant assessment of symptoms and impairments. Of the individuals who initially screened positive on symptom checklists (average age 24), 95% were not diagnosed with ADHD because the symptoms in most cases could be better explained by heavy substance abuse or another mental disorder. The authors also noted that some apparent adult-onset ADHD cases may represent previously well-managed cases of ADHD or sub-threshold ADHD which become problematic for the first time because the individual is encountering increasing performance demands and/or decreasing environmental supports during the course of development such as beginning college (Brown, 2017; Solanto, 2018). In sum, there is grave doubt about the validity of adult-onset ADHD.

Impairments in Life Domains

ADHD has been linked to increased risk for adverse outcomes in virtually every domain that has been studied. These include increased risk for teenage pregnancy and parenthood (Ostergaard, Dalsgaard, Faraone, Munk-Olsen, & Laursen, 2017), a variety of health problems (Barkley, 2015f), injuries (Chien et al., 2017), motor vehicle accidents (Curry et al., 2017), self-harm (females) [Hinshaw, 2018], mortality (Dalsgaard et al., 2015), posttraumatic stress disorder (Spencer et al., 2016), substance abuse (Asherson, 2017; Eme, 2016; Wilens & Morrison, 2015) and an array of psychiatric disorders (Owens et al., 2015). These adverse outcomes have a substantial economic impact. For instance, in the United States annual ADHD-related health care sector costs range from $21 to $44 billion and educational sector costs from $15 to $25 billion (Doshi et al., 2012).

This chapter will focus on impairments in social (family and peer), educational, and occupational settings as they have been found to be among the most important predictors of criminal offending (Farrington, 2012; Nguyen & Loughran, 2018; Savage, Ferguson, & Flores, 2017).

Family

Reviews of research studying parent-child interactions in families of children with ADHD have consistently found that these interactions are characterized by high levels of conflict (Johnston & Chronis-Tuscano, 2015). The fulcrum of the conflict stems from children being criticized or punished repeatedly or harshly for failures they cannot adequately control (Brown, 2017).

> *"Why do you always keep doing what I've asked you repeatedly to stop doing?" "You keep promising that you will write down your assignments in your plan book, and then you keep coming home without doing it!" "Why should I keep helping you with your homework when you don't even bother to hand it in and get credit for it?" "You spend hours intensely focused on playing your video games, but claim you can't focus for just 20 minutes on doing your social studies homework."*
>
> **Brown (2017, p.90)**

The intense and repeated frustration experienced by parents combined with the push back from their children can "set off a chain of reactions and counter reactions that can last a lifetime" (Hinshaw & Ellison, 2016, p. 37). This in turn is highly likely to increase the child's initial impulsive, irritable behavior, thereby promoting the development of antisocial behavior (Hinshaw, 2018).

Peers

ADHD impairs peer relationships in multiple ways (McQuade & Hoza, 2015; Ros & Graziano, 2018). Children with ADHD tend to be more disruptive and intrusive, engaging in behaviors such as interrupting, talking excessively, noisiness, and difficulty waiting turn that peers find highly annoying. Their inattentiveness impairs listening as well as noticing and responding effectively to social cues. They are also more likely to bully and be bullied. The toxic combination of poor academic and social skills results in as many as 50-80% experiencing peer rejection (McQuade & Hoza, 2015). Children who experience peer rejection are more prone to turn to other rejected peers as friends who are more likely to model and encourage antisocial behavior (McQuade & Hoza, 2015). Remarkably, this *deviancy training* can begin on the kindergarten playground where there is minimal adult monitoring (Dishion, Kim & Tein, 2016). Through this association, these young children continue to learn an "antisocial grammar (i.e., being tough wins; deviant behavior is funny)" which culminates in self-organizing into deviant peer groups (e.g., gangs) in early adolescence (Dishion et al., 2016, p. 304).

Education

Children who have problems with attention and organization are likely to experience educational difficulties. Hinshaw and Ellison (2016, p.66) succinctly describe some of the initial difficulties.

> Normally it's by second grade, when teachers first start getting serious about academics and assigning homework, that children with ADHD start to get into real trouble. They can forget to write down their homework assignments, become too distracted to finish them, or, even more frustrating, complete the work but leave it at home on the day that it is due. They find anything else to be more interesting and exciting than listening to the teacher or paying attention during reading circle.

At more advanced levels of education working memory impairments can compound problems caused by inattention as illustrated in the following vignette of a young adult male in doctoral clinical psychology program.

> *When the professor is lecturing and I'm trying to take notes, he'll say one thing and then move on to another. While I am trying to jot that one thing down, as he's still talking, if he moves into the next thing, I can't remember what he transitions into or what he said previously. I mean, maybe I'll forget parts of the phrases and my notes are kind of incomplete because I can't remember the second part of what he just said. It's so frustrating when I study hard for test and then can't remember what I learned. I'll study hard and learn everything. My friends quiz me and I've got it all down. And then when I'm actually taking the test, a big chunk of what I knew so well the night before just evaporates... Then a few hours later it's all back again. It was in my mind. I just couldn't retrieve it.*
>
> **Author's Case**

Not surprisingly, these difficulties, as well as the subsequent development of conduct problems triggered by ADHD, contribute to a cascade of impairments in many aspects of education. For highly intelligent students, problems may not appear until they move from elementary to middle, high school, or college. As they progress they are required to become gradually solely responsible in meeting increasingly complex educational requirements as parental support/structuring of necessity diminishes (Brown, 2017). The problems include lower academic achievement, grade retention, fewer years of education, and more school-related discipline problems (DuPaul & Langberg, 2015; Owens et al., 2015). The impairments can be quite striking. For example, more than half will end up failing at least one grade (Hinshaw & Ellison,

2016), and as many as 46% may be suspended from school (Barkley, 2015g). The emerging literature on college students reports similar findings (Gormley, DuPaul, Weyandt, & Anastopolous, 2016). One aspect of education has seen an improvement. Recent studies have found a decrease in the dropout rate with 10% or fewer failing to complete high school compared with earlier rates of 25% to 40% (Barkley, 2016a). This decline is most likely due to the greater access to special education services than in the past. The increased risk for significant academic and educational attainment problems may also be partly due to comorbid learning disabilities (Owens et al., 2015), and children with ADHD having a lower IQ than those without ADHD (Weyandt & Gudmundsdottir, 2015).

Three mechanisms have been proposed through which educational impairments can increase risk for criminal offending (Savage et al., 2017; Wertz et al., 2018a). First, school problems are likely to engender frustration and negative emotions which play a role in much aggressive and violent behavior. Second, these same problems are likely to weaken school attachment which has been found to protect against crime through commitment to school and its social norms. Third, less schooling may leave juveniles with fewer legitimate methods to achieve wealth or status, increasing incentives to pursue crime.

Occupation

Problems in occupational functioning are pervasive among adults with ADHD (Rooney & Pfiffner, 2018). As reviewed by Barkley (2015f), these include: lower job status; fewer working hours per week; more likely to be fired or experience disciplinary actions; more problems with work performance, punctuality, time management, and maintaining daily responsibilities. These problems likely contribute to numerous financial problems such as higher rates of financial stress, lower earnings, and greater dependence on state welfare systems and family members (Rooney & Pfiffner, 2018). In addition, these problems adversely affect job stability which has consistently been found to be strongly correlated with criminal behavior (Apel & Horney, 2017). Stable employment, like marriage can be a true "turning point" in a criminal career (Nguyen & Loughran, 2018). Strong ties to work can override temptations to engage in criminal behavior, structure daily activities, reduce time spent hanging out/partying, and create or strengthen bonds to law-abiding individuals (Apel & Horney, 2017; Nguyen & Loughran, 2018).

Vignette

The multiple impairments associated with ADHD can become quite debilitating as the following vignette will illustrate. And, to anticipate a subsequent chapter, the vignette also offers an example of the profound improvements that treatment with stimulant medication can provide.

David's Story

*David was chronically dysfunctional, highly intelligent, and a few months away from his 26th birthday when he was evaluated for ADHD by the author. At that time, David's mother predicted that her son "**is either going to be in jail or dead by the time he is 26.**" Four years subsequent to this dire prediction, David was flourishing in virtually all aspects of his life.*

David's Development

As presented in his mother's words, David's development exhibited the classic symptoms of ADHD. David was often infuriating as a child. If I asked him to do something, he'd go off to do it, but when I'd turn around to check, it wouldn't be done and he'd be doing something else. His room was always a wreck. When asked to clean it (rather, organize it – pick up things, put them in their places, etc.) he'd start to. I'd poke my head in a while later and he'd be playing with a toy or involved in something else, his room pretty much as it had been. It seemed that organizing his room was just too big a job for David to do. So, I'd help him. Everything was a big deal to get done. I'd be exasperated trying to get him ready for school on time. He'd start to get ready and then would be off doing something else when it was time to go. I felt caught between David and his stepfather, Jack, for example, when he would ask David to do something and it would never happen. David's IQ is very high and so he could do quite well at school, except he didn't. Schoolwork was boring, Projects weren't completed. So, he'd have a "D" or an "F," and then he'd ace the final. He knew the material. It was just boring putting it down on paper. And, he lost things at school, like his notebook and his homework. He was so disorganized. I bought him organizers for his school things, a notebook in which to write down assignments and due dates. Nothing helped. He didn't seem to care. The school realized suddenly as a result of testing that David was "gifted" and put him in their gifted program. Then I'd get calls that David wasn't completing the assignments required by the gifted program and was on the verge of being dropped from the program. Socially, David just didn't fit in with others. I'd sit at the window, watching children walking home from school in twos and threes. David walked alone. While other children played outside together in the summer, David played or watched television alone. In his teens David made one friend he has to this day. He became more sociable and had girlfriends and other friends – but they didn't seem to last.

David's mother continues with her recollection of David's development into adolescence. David's self-esteem was very low. As a youngster he talked about dying. In his teens he attempted suicide by taking over-the-counter sleeping medication and was twice treated in psychiatric hospitals with no positive results. David's situation worsened.

David was an angry young man and tension was high between him and Jack and me. I couldn't understand why my gifted son couldn't "get his act together." He became extremely aggressive at home to the point where police intervention was required. He was asked to leave home at the age of 18.

He lived in California with my brother until, after several suicide threats, he came home to find David sitting in the living room, holding a wine glass filled with Liquid-Plumber. David returned to his home state, lived with his girlfriend, had a son, and married. Then his wife left him and his infant son. David attempted suicide by taking an overdose of Tylenol. He lost one job, started another, and lost it because he couldn't handle "down time" when working as a radio dispatcher. He'd have what he described as panic attacks. Social relationships were a problem, starting out intense and then dissolving into misunderstanding and conflict. David didn't understand why girlfriends ended their relationships with him.

David lost his apartment, lost his car, couldn't support his son, and slept on the couch in his friend's apartment until he could no longer stay there. David told me that he was disintegrating and that he was making plans for his funeral. He then moved in with his stepfather and me.

David complained of "panic attacks" and "heart problems," reporting that his heart had stopped several times (he had previously gone to the ER by ambulance because of these feelings). His first day with us he had an "attack," which manifested itself in David experiencing shortness of breath and holding his chest while gasping. I called the doctor, but David said he was "fine now." I took David to a heart specialist. No abnormalities were found. Since he had no job and no money, I suggested he go to Family Services for therapy (they have a sliding scale). The psychiatrist suspected, based on David's verbalized symptoms, a seizure disorder and suggested neurological testing, which David could not afford.

Back Home and Sliding Fast

David's mother explains how she and her husband struggled to make sense of David's behavior after he returned home to live.

At home for the first time in years, our adult son's behaviors were shocking. His room was such a mess that there was no clear floor space on which to walk to put a telephone message on his nightstand. I'd step on papers on the floor and then hear the crack of a tape underneath. Layers of things covered the floor, including money and dirty dishes. His bed was never made. Important items were lost in there but he refused to clean it up.

When Jack asked David to input data on his computer, David couldn't do it – making mistake after mistake. Then he'd go upstairs and sit at his computer for five or six hours at a time playing games – doing things he wanted to do. So Jack declared David to be lazy and selfish. David lost important items constantly such as keys, papers and phone numbers. He left on a trip to Connecticut with a friend without enough money to make it back home.

*I knew something was really wrong but couldn't figure out what it was. For example, why would a 25-year-old young man who had a child, didn't have a job, or a real plan for getting a job or an apartment, even though he had a deadline for how long he could live with us, sit for six hours at a stretch at his computer and then go out drinking with friends? David always had an answer, however, for anyone who asked about his plans. He was going to California in August to live and go to school. However, he had no money, no plans, nor any apparent inclination to work. He wasn't realistic. Although his "health problems" decreased without reinforcement, he was in limbo and not functioning competently, apparently not "able" to be self-sufficient. I was afraid that when David left us he would be unable to keep things "together," go downhill, and would wind up homeless, hospitalized, **in jail,** or dead.*

Finally: David's Diagnosis

David's mother continues with the story of how she learned that ADHD could explain many of her son's problems.

Then, I was in an "Eme" class (author's note: the mother was a student of mine), listening to a lecture on ADHD. I'd completed my readings and had listened intently throughout the lecture. However, it wasn't until the last few minutes of class that it hit me like a lightning bolt – ADHD was David's problem! It explained so much of David's troubles. And while I thought it might not be the total "answer," I believed that it was the foundation upon which David's "out of control" life had been built. The whole drive home from school my heart was in my throat. I arrived home, dragged David off his computer and said, "David, I think I know what the problem is."

The formal diagnostic evaluation was conducted shortly thereafter and a regimen of stimulant medication was begun. Note that there was not any other form of intervention other than medication. David was resistant, probably because his experience of about two decades of intermittent psychotherapy, which had been utterly worthless, left him feeling highly skeptical.

David Four Years After Diagnosis and Treatment: A New Life
Recall that at the time of the diagnosis, David's chronically dysfunctional life was on the verge of culminating in jail and/or death. The situation was essentially hopeless despite numerous prior intensive interventions that were oblivious to the existence of the disorder. In the words of David's mother: Prior to David's diagnosis of ADHD, I believed that David's future was bleak, that he would probably spend his days depressed and dependent upon others, unable to eke out a living for himself and his young son. David saw only a downhill course and talked often of death. Then David was correctly diagnosed and treated with Ritalin.

Four years later he is well, functioning in work and in his personal/interpersonal life. He is happy, often euphoric, with a delightful sense of humor; his cup is always half full. This description of a 29- year-old man may be typical of many middle-class young adults in the mid-1990s. For me, however, David's mother, this description of David's current level and quality of functioning is akin to a miracle. David is alive and well, with a positive attitude and a bright future. I believe that this would not have been possible without an accurate diagnosis of ADHD and appropriate treatment.

David's ADHD, which now appears to have been so obvious, had been missed completely by mental health practitioners (psychotherapists, psychologists, and psychiatrists) who had assessed and treated David in his teens and early twenties in mental health clinics and hospitals. His ADHD diagnosis, at age 25, offered David a glimmer of hope-against-hope, a hope he was almost afraid to acknowledge. It provided him with the knowledge that he wasn't "bad" or a "loser" who was unable to function properly or "crazy." It meant he wasn't "losing it!"

Finally, David realized that something physical was wrong with him, a disability that he'd struggled with, in essence, all of his life. He realized that he was no longer to blame for not behaving as everyone thought he should, that his and others' anger directed at him was misdirected. Because it wasn't "him" that was the problem. Those days were over. He could now attribute his many "failures" to something outside of "himself," in the physical realm not within his control. David's hope for a better future became real for him within one hour following Ritalin treatment. He remembers feeling "calm," a feeling he'd never experienced before, a feeling he enjoys to this day. David on Ritalin was different from how he had always been before. David likens taking Ritalin to "putting on mind glasses." He says, "It's like everything's more in focus." He calls it "a different way of being."

Author's Case

CHAPTER FOUR

CRIME

The preceding chapter presented evidence that ADHD can be an important risk factor for criminality via its adverse effects on developmental outcomes that in turn are linked to risk for criminality. This chapter will present evidence from longitudinal studies that directly implicates ADHD as a major risk factor for criminal outcome which results in a prevalence of ADHD among offenders that significantly exceeds the prevalence in the general population. Next, the chapter will explain how this criminal outcome can be understood in terms of a developmental pathway from ADHD to criminal behavior and the environmental risk factors that propel progression along the pathway. The chapter will conclude with descriptions of how ADHD might present in various criminal justice settings.

ADHD and Risk of Criminal Offending

A risk factor can be defined as any influence, whether external to the individual or a characteristic of the individual, that is associated with/predicts the increased probability that a negative outcome will be observed (Compas et al., 2017). The association can be evaluated through longitudinal studies which will be reviewed in this chapter. To establish that the association causes the outcome, it must also be shown that manipulation of the risk factor changes the outcome (Rutter & Thapar, 2016). This can be done either by inducing or removing the risk factor and observing the effect on outcome. Of course, in the case of ADHD, it is not ethically permissible to induce ADHD, even if it were possible to do so. However, as will be discussed in a subsequent chapter, removal of ADHD can be simulated through studying the effects of treatment of ADHD with stimulant medication.

Longitudinal Studies

The major studies that have been identified as having the soundest methodological designs will be reviewed chronologically (Hechtman, 2017; Owen et al., 2015). Although the diagnosis of ADHD in all the reviewed studies antedated the DSM-5, an examination of the criteria used for the diagnosis indicates that most of the children would have qualified for a DSM-5 diagnosis of ADHD-combined presentation (Hechtman, 2017) Thus, while the original terminology of the studies in describing the subjects will be retained (e.g., hyperactivity), the reader should make the appropriate translation.

Los Angeles Study

Beginning in the early 1970's James Satterfield and his colleagues began recruiting white boys (aged 6-12) from consecutive referrals to a psychiatric outpatient clinic in Los Angeles, California specializing in the treatment of hyperactive children for a study of delinquent outcomes and preventative measures (Satterfield et al., 2007). At a 30-year follow-up (average age 18 to 38 years), the study compared the official arrest records of the hyperactive boys (N=179) with control boys (N=75). After controlling for intelligence and socioeconomic status, the hyperactive boys had a higher rate of adult felony arrests (37%), convictions (28%), and incarcerations (25%) than the control group whose rates were 9% (felony arrests), 6% (convictions), and 6% (incarcerations). The best predictor of criminal outcome was comorbid conduct problems (CP). Hyperactive boys without comorbid CP were not at increased risk for later criminality.

New York Study

From 1970 to 1977 a sample of 207 white, middle class hyperactive 6 to 12 year old children was ascertained from over 1000 children who were referred to a psychiatric clinic in New York City (Housais, Hechtman, & Klein, 2017; Mannuzza, Klein, & Moulton, 2008). Children who had a diagnosis of conduct disorder (CD) were excluded as the goal of research was to study *pure* hyperactivity. At age 38 the study focused on the subjects who had lived in New York state throughout the follow-up as their official criminal records were judged to be comprehensive and accurate. Life time criminality was assessed for the 93 male ADHD subjects and a comparison group of 93. Significantly more ADHD subjects than comparisons had been arrested (47% vs 24%), convicted (42% vs.

14%), incarcerated (15% vs 1%), and diagnosed with antisocial personality disorder (ASPD) (23% vs 2%). The increased risk for criminal behavior was completely explained by the development of an antisocial or substance use disorder in adolescence. Thus, even in the absence of clinically diagnosed comorbid CD (although some CD symptoms were present) in childhood, ADHD was found to increase the risk for antisocial and substance use disorders in adolescence. This, in turn, increased the risk for criminal behavior in adolescence and adulthood.

Denmark Study

Dalsgaard, Mortensen, Frydenberg, and Thomsen (2013) identified the case records of 206 children aged 4-15 (181 boys) referred to a psychiatric clinic in Denmark between 1968 and 1989 who were diagnosed with ADHD. Official criminal conviction data was collected on all of them at the average age of 31 and compared with the conviction rates of an age-matched general population sample. Children with ADHD had a 47% (50.3% male, 24% female) conviction rate compared to 7.5% (6.2% male, 1.3% female) in the general population. Comorbid childhood CD doubled the risk for later criminality. Also, similar to the findings in the New York study, ADHD was found to increase the risk for criminal behavior even in the absence of any CD symptoms, as 26% of these children had a criminal conviction.

Milwaukee Study

Between 1979 and 1980 Russell Barkley and his colleagues recruited and enrolled 158 hyperactive children, mostly white males ages 4-12, who were referred to a university medical clinic in Milwaukee, Wisconsin (U.S.) along with a community control group (N=81) [Barkley et al., 2008]. A follow-up which was conducted at the mean age of 27 consisted of 135 of the original hyperactive group and 75 of the controls. The hyperactive group was subdivided into those who retained a diagnosis of ADHD (H+) and those who had either remitted or had borderline cases of ADHD (H-). Both hyperactive groups were more likely to have been arrested (H+ 73%, H- 52%) or jailed (H+58%, H-46%) than the control group (20% arrested, 16% jailed). Also, both the H+ and H- groups had higher rates of ASPD than the comparison group, 39%, 17%, 8% respectively. The best childhood predictors of criminal behavior were the pervasiveness of ADHD symptoms and conduct problems.

Massachusetts Study

In the 1980's Joseph Biederman and his colleagues recruited and enrolled 140 white males and 140 white females (aged 6-17) with ADHD from a pediatric psychopharmacology clinic and from primary care pediatrics practices in the state of Massachusetts (Uchida & Biederman, 2017). The subjects were matched to 120 male and 122 female control children. At a 10-year follow-up (mean age 22), 208 of the ADHD subjects (112 boys, 96 girls) and 196 controls (105 boys, 91 girls) were evaluated for a life-time prevalence of ASPD. The ADHD subjects were far more likely than the controls (39% vs. 8%) to have developed the disorder. Gender did not differentially influence any of the outcomes except perhaps a delay in the onset of disruptive behavior which occurred later in girls than in boys.

Pittsburg Study

The Pittsburg Longitudinal study recruited a sample of 288 mostly white males who had received a diagnosis of ADHD between 1987 and 1996 (ages 5-13, mean=9 years) at a psychiatric clinic in Pittsburgh, Pennsylvania (Sibley et al., 2011) They were followed-up until all the subjects were at least 18 years of age so that a cumulative record of delinquency could be obtained. A comparison group of 209 demographically matched males was also recruited. Delinquency information (severity, variety, and age of initiation) was gathered based on self and parent report. At follow-up, four childhood diagnostic groups (ADHD-only), (ADHD+Oppositional Defiant Disorder), (ADHD+CD), and the comparison group were formed to examine group differences on three delinquency outcomes: severity, age of initiation, and variety. The findings indicated that regardless of comorbidity, all children with ADHD were at some type of risk for delinquency. The clearest finding of the study was that children with ADHD+CD displayed the worst delinquency outcomes compared to the other three groups, across almost all indices. For example, 45% of the boys with ADHD+CD had engaged in at least one episode of severe delinquency compared to 5% of the comparison group, accounting for half of the severe offenders.

Multimodal Treatment Study

In the most recent follow-up of the MTA study (see footnote 13) at a mean age of 25, Hechtman and colleagues (2016) assessed the outcomes of 476 of the ADHD individuals and 241 comparison subjects. No difference was found in either jail time or reported police contact. The finding of no difference in criminality, in contrast to all the preceding studies, may be due to three of the study's limitations noted by the authors. First, 18% of the ADHD subjects lost to follow-up were characterized by a number of risk factors associated with poorer outcome (e.g., lower IQ, more severe ADHD, higher rates of Oppositional Defiant Disorder). Therefore, it is possible that a significant difference in criminal behavior might have been found had these subjects been retained. Second, self-report by the subjects, which was the principal measure on all outcome measures, is commonly acknowledged as being subject to underreporting of criminal behavior. Third, the study did not assess for ASPD.

Prediction of Adolescent Outcomes Among Children Diagnosed with ADHD at 4-6 Years of Age

A study by Lahey and colleagues addressed the problem that little is known about the stability and long-term consequence of ADHD when it is diagnosed in early childhood (Lahey et al., 2016). Participants were 125 children (107 boys) recruited from various mental health settings who were diagnosed with ADHD at 4-6 years and 130 comparison children. The participants were followed prospectively through age 18 years with good retention for both groups. During 15-18 years of age, more children with ADHD were arrested (based upon adolescent and parent report) at least once (30%) than were comparison children (9%). Higher numbers of concurrent CD symptoms in childhood predicted increased risk for delinquency.

Conclusion

The major long-term longitudinal studies of ADHD have clearly established that childhood ADHD is an important risk factor for the development of antisocial/criminal behavior. An estimate of the magnitude of this risk is provided from two sources. First, in her summary of the outcomes of childhood ADHD in the major longitudinal studies, Hechtman (2017) estimated that about 10% to 20% of individuals with childhood ADHD develop significant antisocial problems. Second, Mohn-Jensen and Steinhausen (2016) conducted a systematic review and meta-analysis of the risks of childhood ADHD on long-term outcome of arrests, convictions, and incarceration which included some of the major studies reviewed by Hechtman, an additional number of minor longitudinal studies, and some retrospective studies. They reported that childhood ADHD was associated with a relative risk of 2.2 for arrests, 3.3 for convictions, and 2.9 for incarceration. In addition, individuals with childhood ADHD had a younger age of onset of antisocial behavior and increased risk of criminal recidivism. The most robust baseline predictors of antisocial outcome were comorbid conduct problems and ADHD severity. Persistence of ADHD was also found to be an important predictor.

These conclusions need to be understood in the context of two limitations. First, most of the ADHD subjects were drawn from clinical populations who would be more likely than ADHD subjects in the general populations to have more severe ADHD, as well as associated problems. Thus the risk ADHD poses for future antisocial behavior may have been inflated. Second, the vast majority of the subjects were white males, restricting generalization of these findings to other ethnic groups.

Lastly, and very importantly, many studies, because of the very real concern of confounding variables, having found that ADHD is clearly correlated with an increased risk for criminality, will statistically control for various covariates such as CD. Upon finding that this control either markedly diminishes or completely eliminates the association between ADHD and criminality, the study will minimize the significance of ADHD as a causal risk factor for criminality. For example, most recently van der Mass and colleagues (2018) found that adults who screened positive for ADHD, or reported past use of medication for ADHD, were twice or three times more likely to report ever having been arrested compared to a control group. These associations were no longer significant after statistically controlling for a covariate termed "weak social bonds" as indexed by general antisocial behavior, drug use, failure to progress educationally, etc. Therefore, they concluded that the association between ADHD and criminality is best understood through their shared association with weak social bonds. However, if behaviors develop as a consequence of ADHD, the statistical controls are not appropriate. As Rutter and Thapar (2016) point out: "It would be inappropriate to control for factors (e.g., social bonds)[1] that are intermediate on the pathway between exposure to the risk factor (e.g., ADHD) and the outcome (e.g., criminality) or those that are caused in part by exposure to the risk experience (e.g., general antisocial behavior, drug use, failure to progress educationally)" (p.131). This is precisely the case with ADHD as will

[1] The examples were inserted into the quote.

subsequently be discussed when a developmental pathway from ADHD to criminality is presented.

Prevalence of ADHD in Prison Populations

Studies report prison prevalence rates of ADHD ranging from 9% to 50% (Murphy & Appelbaum, 2017). This mirrors the wide variation in prevalence rates found in studies in the general population (Thomas et. al., 2015). And, as with studies of the general population, the best solution to such variability is to conduct a systematic review and meta-analysis of prison studies of ADHD prevalence to arrive at a reliable estimate. Such an estimate has been provided in a meta-analysis of 42 international studies (Young, Moss, Sedgwick, Fridman, & Hodgkins, 2015) which reported a prevalence of 21.7%. It also found that youth prevalence rates were not significantly different from estimates for adults, nor were there any significant differences for gender. However, this latter finding may not be reliable as there were only a few data sets reporting on female prevalence. The estimate was based upon the typical protocol used in the studies of ADHD prevalence in the general population, i.e., standardized interview conducted by trained interviewers.

It is highly likely that the true prison prevalence rate of ADHD is significantly higher than 21.7%. As previously discussed, the methods that have typically been used to assess population prevalence, which are the similar to those used to assess prison prevalence, will tend to significantly underestimate true prevalence because they for the most part used less sensitive DSM-IV criteria. Most importantly, the studies of the prevalence of ADHD in prisons did not collect information from collateral informants. This failure, as previously discussed, has been found to vastly underestimate ADHD prevalence. In addition, inmates may be less likely to report ADHD symptoms and impairments because the "structure, routine, and predictability of their daily schedule" reduces the likelihood of their occurrence" (Murphy & Appelbaum, 2017, p.4). On the other hand, some of the characteristics of prison populations such as traumatic life events, comorbid disorders, and substance use disorders can mimic ADHD symptoms which even trained interviewers who are not professionals may misinterpret for ADHD (Murphy & Appelbaum, 2017). Overall though, it would seem that the factors increasing the possibility of underdiagnosis, especially the crucial failure to use collateral informants, would decisively outweigh the factors increasing the possibility of overdiagnosis.

In summary, in view of the preceding considerations, the meta-analytic finding of 21.7% ADHD prevalence among incarcerated males would seem to be an underestimate. A more accurate, conservative estimate would be 25%. The magnitude of this prevalence, which is approximately three times greater than the population prevalence for adult males, conclusively establishes the importance of identifying and treating ADHD in prison populations. A developmental pathway that explains how ADHD increases risk for criminality will now be presented.

A Developmental Pathway to Criminality

A developmental pathway refers to a sequence and timing of behavioral continuities and transformations across development with individuals differing in their propensity to progress along the successive behavior represented by the pathway. Progress along the pathway is probabilistic, not deterministic (Hayden & Mash, 2014). A developmental pathway model proposed by Beauchaine and colleagues (Beauchaine, & McNulty, 2013; Beauchaine, Shader, & Hinshaw, 2016; Beauchaine, Zisner, & Sauder, 2017; Neuhaus & Beauchaine, 2017;; Zisner & Beauchaine, 2016a,b) which explains how ADHD increases risk for criminality will now be presented. The model is based on findings from numerous studies that early-starting male antisocial behavior that tends to be life course persistent[2] can begin with a biologically-based vulnerability to the temperamental trait of impulsivity whose extreme expression early in life takes the form of the hyperactive-impulsive and combined presentations of ADHD[3] (Beauchaine & Hinshaw, 2016; Beauchaine, & McNulty, 2013; Beauchaine et al., 2016, 2017; Martel, Levinson, Lee, & Smith, 2017; Neuhaus & Beauchaine, 2017; Rodenacker, Hautmann, Gortz-Dorlen, & Dopfner, 2018; Zisner & Beauchaine, 2016a,b). Subsequently, ADHD can interact and transact with various environmental adversities that can result in escalating rates of antisocial behavior

---

[2] In 1993 Terrie Moffitt proposed a developmental taxonomy of antisocial behavior that has been validated by a quarter of a century of research (Moffit, 2006, 2018), thereby making it one of the most influential of all developmental theories of antisocial behavior (Piquero, Gonzalez, & Jennings, 2015). In this theory, there is a type of extreme and pervasive antisocial behavior, almost exclusively male, that persists from early childhood to adulthood, i.e., tends to be life-course-persistent (LCP). The risk for LCP emerges from inherited and acquired neuropsychological problems such as hyperactivity.

[3] The discussion of ADHD in the pathway model will always refer to these presentations unless otherwise indicated.

culminating in criminality. More than a half a century ago Lee Robins (1966, 1978) published a landmark study *Deviant Children Grown Up: A Sociological and Psychiatric Study of Sociopathic Personality* which presented the findings of a 30-year follow-up of 524 white juveniles (73% male) most of whom were referred for antisocial behavior to a child guidance clinic in the 1920's. This study proved to be of paramount importance for the succeeding 50 years of the study of criminality with her most seminal finding arguably being that severe adult antisocial behavior virtually requires childhood antisocial behavior (Moffitt, 2018). Specifically, abundant research triggered by Robins influential finding has found that adult antisocial males commonly follow a developmental pathway that "begins as early as preschool with hyperactivity/impulsivity and oppositionality, followed by conduct problems in middle school, delinquency and substance use in high school, and incarceration and recidivism by late adolescence and adulthood" (Beauchaine & Hinshaw, 2016, p.xvii). These findings, translated into the DSM-5 classification system, mean that males who develop criminal behavior usually traverse a developmental pathway that spans the spectrum of externalizing disorders[4] beginning in early childhood with ADHD, followed by Oppositional Defiant Disorder (ODD), child-onset Conduct Disorder (CD), Substance Use Disorders (SUDs), culminating in Antisocial Personality Disorder (ASPD) [Beauchaine & Hinshaw, 2016; Beauchaine, & McNulty, 2013; Beauchaine et al., 2016, 2017]. Similarly, one of the foremost criminologists, Adrian Raine (2018), has recently proposed that both child-onset CD and APD both be considered neurodevelopmental disorders, while also observing that those with APD often have a history of ADHD. Thus, "it seems that different researchers, from different perspectives, are converging on a similar theme" (Raine, personal communication, 5/21/18). Indeed, "This developmental pathway may account for most individuals who engage in lifelong delinquent behavior" (Beauchaine et al., 2017, p. 345), i.e., LCP. Not all youth with ADHD progress along the pathway to more severe forms of antisocial behavior, but there clearly is a subset of youth with ADHD who can become

[4] The term *externalizing* and its counterpart *internalizing* are widely used in the psychopathology literature to describe two broad groupings of behavioral, emotional, and social problems (Achenbach, 2016). The externalizing group represents disorders with prominent impulsive, disruptive conduct, and substance use symptoms The internalizing group represents disorders with prominent anxiety, depressive, and somatic symptoms.

embroiled in various adverse environments and advance along such a pathway.

It is important to note that this developmental progression should not be thought of as an individual with ADHD accumulating a host of unrelated comorbid disorders (ODD, CD, SUD). There is rampant comorbidity (i.e., the co-occurrence of two or more disorders in the same individual at the same time, Clark et al., 2017) in mental-disorder diagnoses, most of which is artefactual (i.e., comorbidity derived by mistakenly splitting one disorder into multiple diagnoses) or spurious (i.e., comorbidity resulting from shared diagnostic criteria across different disorders) (Beauchaine & McNulty, 2013; Clark et al., 2017). True comorbidity refers to the random co-occurrence of two or more independent disorders in the same person at the same time (Clark et al., 2017). As such, truly independent disorders not only have distinct signs and symptoms, but also different etiologies (Clark et al., 2017). For example, a person may have the flu and appendicitis. On the other hand, comorbid disorders may also be linked while still being clearly distinct as when, for example, kidney disease develops as a complication of diabetes (Clark et al., 2017). The developmental model of a progression from ADHD to criminality developed by Beauchaine and colleagues reflects this understanding of comorbidity. It is referred to as an "ontogenic process" (Beauchaine et al., 2017, p. 358), i.e., a development unfolding of increasingly more severe antisocial behaviors that results from interactions and transactions between the vulnerability conferred by ADHD and various environmental risk factors. Beauchaine and colleagues (2017) have likened this ontogenic process to that of the vulnerability impaired glucose intolerance poses for the eventual outcome of type II diabetes. This vulnerability, interacting with environmental risk factors, can result in a course that "begins with insulin resistance, which is followed by a host of increasingly adverse sequelae, including weigh gain, elevated triglycerides, high blood pressure, nonalcoholic fatty liver disease, inflammation, ischemic heart disease, kidney failure, retinal damage, and peripheral neuropathy" (Beauchaine et al., 2017, p. 358). Thus, it would not be proper to characterize an individual who is in an advanced stage of diabetes as having been so unfortunate as to have been suffered the random co-occurrence of several unrelated disorders. Similarly, it would not be proper to characterize an individual who, beginning with ADHD, is in an advanced stage (i.e., criminality) of the proposed antisocial pathway as having randomly acquired a multitude of unrelated antisocial disorders. To do so would obscure the underlying causal mechanism and continuity among the disorders (Hinshaw, 2017,

2018). This ontogenic process exemplifies what in the lexicon of developmental psychology is termed *heterotypic continuity* (Hinshaw, 2017, 2018). Namely, the sequential development of increasingly more severe antisocial disorder reflects different manifestations (i.e., heterotypic) of an underlying continuing vulnerability (i.e., ADHD). In short, the 25% of individuals in the criminal justice system with ADHD are best conceptualized as being in an advanced antisocial stage which began with ADHD.

The developmental pathway from ADHD to criminal behavior and the environmental risk factors that propel progression along the pathway will now be presented.

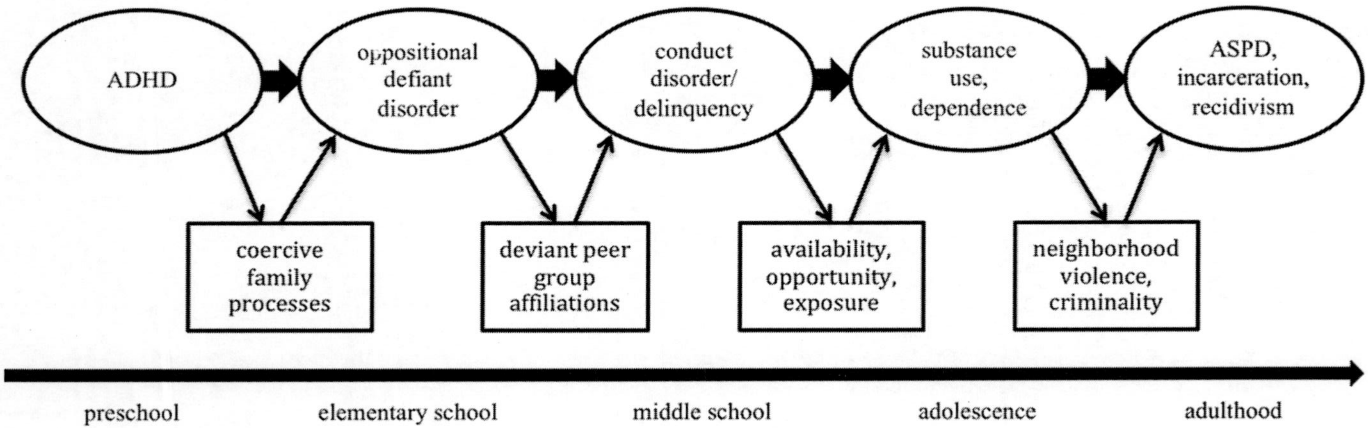

Adapted with copyright permission from T. Beauchaine

Figure 4-1

Attention-Deficit/Hyperactivity Disorder

As discussed earlier, ADHD is best understood as a global self-regulation disorder involving attention, behavior, and emotion. It is this pervasive dysregulation that explains why ADHD can be a core predisposing vulnerability to all of the increasingly severe antisocial disorders across development mentioned above, beginning with ODD. As Barkley (2015c, p.100) has noted, children with ADHD "could be considered to be virtually borderline or subthreshold cases of ODD as a consequence" of their emotional impulsivity. Their low frustration tolerance, impatience, and quickness to anger increases the likelihood of coercive interactions initially with parents. This can result in the learning of oppositional and defiant behaviors either because of lax, inconsistent parenting or harsh parenting (Danforth, Connor, & Doerfler, 2016); Hinshaw & Ellison, 2016. For example, in the case of parental laxity, a coercive interchange may ensue when a parent presents a child with a direction that the child defies, opposes. If the parent acquiesces to the defiance, the child will learn that such behavior is effective through a learning mechanism of negative reinforcement. In this mechanism, a behavior (defiance) allows the child to escape or avoid a negative situation (parental direction) which thereby reinforces the defiant behavior. In a second scenario, if the parent reacts to the child's defiance with a harsh, punitive response, this can make the child even more angry and aggressive (Hinshaw & Ellison, 2016) through the mechanisms of imitation and frustration aggression (Eisner & Malti, 2015). For example, a recent longitudinal study of preschool children with ADHD found increases in argumentative/ defiant ODD symptoms over a three-year period (Harvey, Lugo-Candelas, & Breaux, 2015; Harvey, Breaux, & Lugo-Candelas, 2016). Thus, progression along the pathway from ADHD to ODD is extremely common, especially in severe cases of ADHD (Barkley, 2015c). ODD occurs on average in 65% of community cases and in as many as 85% of clinic-referred cases of child ADHD (Barkley, 2015c). Additional evidence that ADHD increases risk for ODD is found in the studies of the effects of ADHD medications on both ADHD and ODD symptoms. As reviewed by Barkley (2016a), research has found that reductions in ADHD symptoms produced by such medications are accompanied by nearly equal reductions in ODD symptoms. Yet these medications have little, if any, effect on ODD when it occurs separately from ADHD.

Oppositional Defiant Disorder

Oppositional Defiant Disorder is a common and impairing disruptive disorder and a leading cause of referral for youth for mental health services (Demmer, Hooley, Sheen, Mcgillivary, & Lum, 2017; Nock, Kazdin, Hiripi, & Kessler, 2007; Lahey & Waldham, 2017; Zastrow, Martel, & Widiger, 2016). ODD is characterized by a pattern of angry, hostile, and/or defiant behaviors and interactions with others (APA, 2013). In addition, several recent studies have found that ODD symptoms can be partitioned into two different symptom dimensions: angry/irritable (e.g., "being touchy, angry," and "often loses temper") and argumentative/defiant (e.g., "argues," "defies," and is "spiteful/vindictive") [Burke et al., 2014; Herzhoff & Tackett, 2016; Lahey & Waldham, 2017; Zastrow et al., 2016]. Thus, ODD can be best understood as a disorder with two specific related and not entirely independent components (Burke et al., 2014).

Furthermore, the progression of ADHD to ODD is frequently accompanied by the ominous development of physical aggression (Tremblay, Vitaro, & Cote, 2018). The Quebec Longitudinal Study of Child Development, with a large population-based sample of approximately 2000 children, found that 10% of boys and 3.7% of girls were on a stable trajectory for high levels of hyperactivity-impulsivity, non-compliance, or physical aggression from age 1 ½ to 5 years (Carbonneau, Boiven, Brendgen, Nagin, & Tremblay, 2016). In a subsequent follow-up of these children (Pingualt et al., 2013), hyperactivity, inattention, and physical aggression were annually assessed between the ages of 6 and 12 years. Criminality by age 25 was assessed from official court records. Physical aggression was found to be the single most important predictor of criminality. Children (mostly males) who were on a high trajectory for physical aggression (based on mother/teacher ratings) accounted for 45.9% of all recorded criminal charges and 57.4% of the violent ones. The importance of these findings is further underscored by the fact that preschool children who do not demonstrate high levels of hyperactivity-impulsivity, oppositionality and physical aggression are unlikely to progress to more severe antisocial behaviors (Shaw, 2013). The extent to which preschool children do exhibit these behaviors readily explains why ODD's role as a developmental precursor to CD is well documented with approximately 25% or more of children with ODD going on to develop CD (Kimonis, Frick, & McMahon, 2014; Lahey & Waldham, 2017). It is now understood that ODD (especially the argumentative/defiant dimension) plays a key role in the development of CD and is one of the strongest predictors of child-onset CD (Loeber, Burke, & Pardini, 2009; Stringaris & Goodman, 2009). Although the majority of children with ODD do not go on to develop CD (Loeber et al., 2009), if childhood-onset CD develops, it is almost always preceded developmentally by ODD (Burke, Waldham, & Lahey, 2010).

Conduct Disorder

According to the DSM-5, CD is defined as "A repetitive pattern of behavior in which the basic rights of others or major age-appropriate societal norms or rules are violated..." (APA, 2013, p. 469). Strongly influenced by the landmark review paper of Terrie Moffitt (1993), DSM-IV and DSM-5 have parsed antisocial youth into two groups of early-onset and adolescent-onset CD (Lahey & Waldham, 2017). Youth who develop early-onset CD are much more likely than those with adolescent-onset to engage in more serious antisocial behaviors and to persist in such behavior into adulthood (Moffitt, 2018; Lahey & Waldham, 2017). Indeed, "It is axiomatic that criminal career extremity is inversely related to onset..." (DeLisi, & Piquero, 2011). Unsurprisingly then, a wealth of evidence links CD to numerous poor outcomes, including SUD (Erskine et al., 2016; Raine, 2018; Wertz et al., 2018b). The progression to SUD can be explained as reflecting a generalized proneness to engage in deviant behaviors of all kinds, including substance abusing behaviors (Brown, Tomlinson, & Windward, 2017; Molina & Pelham, 2014).

It should also be noted that ADHD might directly increase the risk for SUD because the impulsive risk taking and sensation seeking associated with ADHD increases the likelihood of experimenting with various substances (Erskine et al., 2016). Wilens and Morrison (2015, p.113) also report that there is "compelling" evidence to support a *self-medication* theory, i.e., substances, licit and illicit, are used to medicate ADHD symptoms. In the MTA study, a group with childhood ADHD followed-up into young adulthood and with persistent substance use (SU) [alcohol, marijuana, and other drugs] was more likely to report that SU (specifically marijuana) enhanced positive mood and reduced negative mood, calming hyperactive-impulsive symptoms, than those who desisted from substance use (both those with ADHD and a normal comparison group [Mitchell et al., 2018]. The ADHD group with persistent SU (again, specifically cannabis) was also more likely than the normal comparison group with persistent SU to give *stability* as a reason for use (Swanson et al., 2018). Stability was defined as engaging in SU to achieve a more stable functioning in life (including *self-medication*, relief of anxiety, stress, etc.).What renders these perceptions of benefit plausible is that all known addictive drugs activate reward regions in the brain by causing sharp increases in dopamine (Volkow, Koob, & McClellan, 2016). Increasing the level of dopamine is the major mechanism whereby treatment with stimulant medication for ADHD exerts its efficacy, as will subsequently be discussed (Faraone et al., 2015).

Substance Use Disorder

Substance use disorders in adolescence involve self-administration of any substance that induces long term changes in mood, perception, or brain function (Brown, Tomlinson, & Winward, 2017). As rates of alcohol, cigarette, and marijuana use are very low prior to age 11, the critical period for substance abuse is from eight to twelfth grade when rates increase dramatically (van Emmerick-van Oortmerssen, 2012). Individuals with childhood ADHD compared to those without are more likely to engage in early use of all substances in adolescence and also more likely to have faster increases in alcohol and illicit drug use in adolescence (Molina et al., 2018). Most individuals who have an SUD began their substance use before age 18 (Eiden et al., 2016).

The link between substance abuse (SA) and criminal offending is one of the most reliable findings in criminology (White, 2016). Substance use exacerbates escalation of antisocial behavior (e.g., from minor aggression to violence) among young men (White, Conway, Buckman, & Loeber, 2018). Substance users are more likely to commit crimes than nonusers, and criminal offenders generally report heavier alcohol and drug use than non-offenders (White, 2016). For example, in the U.S., more than two-thirds of offenders may have a substance use disorder at the time of their entry into the criminal justice system (Trestman et al., 2016), and 52% of violent offenders and 39% of property offenders report being under the influence of alcohol or drugs when committing the crime (Miller, Levy, Cohen, & Cox, 2006) The link between substance abuse and criminality is bidirectional, i.e., SA→Crime, and Crime→SA. Substance abuse can increase risk for criminal behavior in several ways: a) acute intoxication increases risk for criminal behavior, b) addiction increases the risk for income generating crime to satisfy the need for expensive drugs, c) addictive substances can further compromise the functioning of the mesolimbic and mesocortical DA networks, thereby amplifying behavioral and emotional impulsivity (Beauchaine et al., 2017; Koob & Volkow, 2016; White, 2016). In addition, the criminal life style can increase risk of SA, as criminal offenders may be more likely than nonoffenders to select, or be pushed into situations or subcultures involving alcohol and drugs (White, 2016).

Criminality

The culminating stage reflects the consistent finding of a marked continuity/stability in antisocial behavior and criminal offending from childhood through adolescence and into adulthood (Farrington & Loeber, 2012). This does not mean that all antisocial children become antisocial adults, as about 50%–70% of individuals with childhood- onset conduct problems outgrow their difficulties by adolescence (Fairchild, Van Goozen, Calder, & Goodyer, 2013). However, it does mean that for the most part adults who engage in criminal behavior virtually always begin as children with antisocial misconduct (Moffitt, 2018). This finding is anchored in extensive research that has identified a group of individuals who are on a life-course-persistent (LCP) trajectory of antisocial behavior. The LCP trajectory is characterized by social, familial, and neurodevelopmental deficits (e.g., ADHD), onsets in early childhood, and continues into adolescence and adulthood when antisocial behaviors become far more serious (Bushway, 2013; Fairchild et al., 2013; Farrington & Loeber, 2012; Kimonis et al., 2014; Moffitt, 2018). For example, the Dunedin study[1] found that 33% of males on the LCP pathway (vs. 0.4% on the low antisocial pathway) were convicted of violent offenses between ages 26 and 32 (Odgers et al., 2008). In the most recent follow-up this study, most LCP men approaching midlife had not desisted from crime; 55% were convicted between ages 26 and 38 years, versus 30% men who had an adolescent onset of CD. In comparison, the prevalence of conviction among all men in the cohort between ages 26 and 38 was 18% (Moffitt, 2018).

Environmental Risk Factors

A number of environmental risk factors propel progression along the pathway from ADHD to criminality. Three of the most important factors as identified by Beauchaine and colleagues (2017) will be reviewed: ineffective parenting and coercive family processes, deviant peer group affiliation, and neighborhood risk.

[1] The Dunedin Multidisciplinary Health and Development study is one of the most important studies in the history of criminology, generating over 1200 publications and reports (Poulton, Moffitt, & Silva, 2015). The study, begun more than 40 years ago, is an ongoing longitudinal investigation of health and behavior (including antisocial behavior) of a complete birth cohort (n=1037) born in Dunedin, New Zealand (Moffitt, 2018).

Ineffective Parenting and Coercive Family Processes

As previously discussed, ADHD symptoms of behavioral and emotional impulsivity greatly increase the risk for conflictual, oppositional interchanges with significant others in the child's life. Indeed, it is estimated that a typical child with ADHD has an astonishing half a million of these negative interchanges each year (Pelham & Fabiano, 2008). Parents in an attempt to manage the child's behavior become excessively critical (Noordermeer et al., 2017) and tend to resort to utilizing various harsh and punitive methods (e.g., yelling, threatening, corporal punishment). In general they are more likely to exhibit ineffectual parenting (i.e., inconsistent, harsh, lax, overreactive, less responsive) compared to parents of children without ADHD (Chacko et al., 2015). This type of parenting is more likely to occur in the 25-35% of parents of ADHD children who themselves have ADHD (Park, Hudec, & Johnston (2017). Consequently, a coercive spiral of more challenging child behaviors and increased harsh and punitive parental behavior can develop in which children learn to use aversive behaviors to obtain rewards or escape parental demands (Snyder, 2016). These coercive family dynamics increase the risk of children with ADHD being more likely to be maltreated by their parents than are typically developing children (Hinshaw & Ellison, 2016). Maltreatment increases the risk for a range of antisocial behaviors including CD, juvenile delinquency and adult crime (Braga, Cumba, & Maia, 2018; Jaffee, 2017; Widom, 2017). This coercive dynamic can then generalize to peer groups (Beauchaine et al., 2017).

Deviant Peer Group

As previously discussed, children with ADHD are more likely to experience peer rejection. Consequently, they are more likely to turn to other rejected peers as friends who are more likely to model and encourage antisocial behavior. This self-organization into deviant peer groups in early adolescence amplifies the existing antisocial behaviors through the twin processes of *deviancy training* and *coercive joining* (Dishion et al., 2016). Deviancy training refers to the reinforcement of various rule-breaking behavior and norms. Coercive joining refers to adolescent gang relationships that are not characterized by typical adolescent friendships of joining and sharing a common interest but by interactions that are abrasive and harsh, with youth treating one another with a mix of coercion and control to attain dominance. Thus, these youths socialize each other to serious antisocial behavior through mutual training in coercion, dominance, and dangerousness.

Neighborhood Risks

Children with ADHD who have developed ODD problems are much more likely to develop more serious antisocial problems when reared in low socioeconomic (SES) neighborhoods characterized by "socioeconomic disadvantages, social disorganization, structural inequality, residential instability, poverty," all of which are indicative of "general neighborhood disorder" (Jennings et al., 2018, p.73; McDonough-Caplan & Beauchaine, in press). This general disorder results in children being more likely to be exposed to frequent violence and stressful life events, a higher density of deviant peers, and more frequent parent-child conflict than children in middle or upper SES neighborhoods (Jennings et al., 2018; McDonough-Caplan & Beauchaine, 2015). In short, neighborhood *disorder* amplifies risk for conduct *disorder* in vulnerable children.

Lastly, it should be noted that high levels of supportive parenting defined as parental monitoring (i.e., the extent to which parents keep track of/monitor their children) and maternal warmth can markedly reduce the risks for antisocial behavior associated with being reared in a lower SES (Jennings et al., 2018; Odgers et al., 2012). For example, Odgers and colleagues (2012) studied the relationship between SES and children's aggressive and delinquent behaviors. The study tracked the development of a nationally representative birth cohort of 2,232 British children through age 12. It found that the large differences in children's levels and rate of change in antisocial behavior across deprived versus more affluent neighborhoods were completely mediated by supportive parenting practices. In other words, the increased risk associated with children being raised in a lower SES versus a middle or upper SES was totally eliminated if the children were raised by supportive parents!

Conclusion

Approximately 25% of males in the criminal justice system have ADHD. The magnitude of this prevalence, which is approximately three times greater than the population prevalence for adult males, conclusively establishes the importance of identifying and treating ADHD in criminal populations. A developmental pathway model that explains this prevalence begins with a biologically-based vulnerability to the temperamental trait of impulsivity whose extreme expression early in life takes the form of the hyperactive-impulsive and combined presentations of ADHD. Subsequently, ADHD can interact and transact with various environmental risk factors such as ineffective parenting, association with deviant peers, and being raised low socioeconomic neighborhoods characterized by general disorder. This can result in escalating rates of antisocial behavior over time such that youth can progress from ADHD through subsequent stages of Oppositional Defiant Disorder, Conduct Disorder, Substance Use Disorder, culminating in criminal behavior.

How ADHD Offenders Might Present in Criminal Justice Settings

The operative word in the section heading is "might" as research on how offenders with ADHD present in criminal justice settings is scant. Hence the following discussion will be largely based on the anecdotal accounts in provided by Patrick Hurley (see footnote #2), supplemented by the extent research. To the extent that there is research, it has mainly been conducted by the Adult ADHD Network in the UK (Young et al., 2011). This network consists of a group of mental health specialists who have experience delivering clinical services for adults with ADHD within the national health service, including criminal justice settings. The following settings will be discussed: police services, court services/ probation and parole, and prison services.

Police Services

Individuals with ADHD can escalate contacts with police and make even minor situations much worse than they need be because of their impulsivity, inattentiveness, and defiance of authority (i.e. ODD). For example, in a routine traffic stop a motorist might ask themselves in rapid and sometimes jumbled order some of the following questions.

- Why am I being followed?
- Just how fast was I going?
- If I am stopped, will I get a ticket?
- How many tickets have I already gotten in the past year?
- Is my driver's license suspended or revoked? Has it expired?
- Have I been drinking?
- Have I had too much to drink?
- Have I been using illegal drugs?

In addition to the normal stresses induced by these questions, the individual with ADHD (let's call him Chris), who is more likely to be stopped than their non-ADHD peer because of their risk taking and distractibility (Barkley, 2015f),

- Is more likely than their non ADHD peer to have a record of speeding, reckless driving, driving under suspension, or driving under the influence of alcohol or drugs (Barkley, 2015f).
- Might have tried to elude police in the past and be thinking about trying it again now.
- Might be angry at himself for once again "messing up" and getting another traffic ticket.
- Most probably had previous problems with authority figures – parents, teachers, other police officers, etc.

All these factors churn in Chris's mind when the officer flicks on the top lights in his patrol car and perhaps activates the siren. When Chris pulls his car over, after being directed to stop, the officer, as trained, approaches the car cautiously and remains observant of the car's occupants – those already visible and those who might be out of view. It's nighttime, so the officer shines a bright spotlight into the rear-view mirror of Chris's car. Chris doesn't know all this. To him, it just feels like an authority figure being aggressive. His anxiety level shot through the roof a few minutes ago, taking his self-control with it, and he just *reacts*. Without thinking, he exits the car, starts pacing in an agitated way, and impulsively blurts out in a rude tone of voice to the officer, "Why did you stop me and what's up with the spotlight in my mirror?"

Caught up in his impulsivity, Chris has just made two huge mistakes, both of which could escalate a simple traffic warning memo into a summons – or worse – not to mention making it look like he's surely guilty of more than running that stop sign. Chris isn't thinking about consequences. Faced with such apparent hostility, a well-trained officer will immediately go on alert. When a motorist exits his car, officers might suspect he is hiding something in his vehicle or is trying to distract the officer's attention while another person in the car is doing something else. If Chris continues to act aggressively or even inappropriately defensive, the situation can slide downhill quickly.

The foregoing scenario can be generalized to any number of different interactions with the police. One of these, for which there is some research, is how individuals with ADHD cope with police interrogations. Two studies have found that individuals with ADHD are more likely than those without ADHD to make a false confession. In the first study, 90

Icelandic prisoners, half of whom met screening criteria for childhood ADHD, were recruited for a study which included the question: "Have you ever made a confession to the police about a crime you did not commit?" (Gudjonsson, Sigurdsson, Bragason, Newton, & Einarsson, 2008). Those with ADHD were significantly more likely those without to report having made a false confession (41% vs. 18%). ADHD was also found to predict false confessions above antisocial personality disorder in this study (Gudjonsson, Sigurdsson, Bragason, Newton, & Einarsson, 2010). In the second study, 22,226 young persons in Iceland completed self-report questionnaires which screened for ADHD and also were asked whether they had ever falsely confessed to a crime during a police interrogation. Those who screened positive for ADHD were 3.7 times more likely to have made a false confession than those who screened negative (Gudjonsson et al., 2016). Among the various reasons for false confessions such as protecting someone else, being under the influence of drugs, succumbing to police pressure, the authors theorized that it may have been the impulsive desire to escape from the stress of interrogation that increased the likelihood of false confession in individuals with ADHD compared to those without ADHD (Gudjonsson et al., 2008).

Court Services/Probation and Parole

ADHD offenders exhibit similar problems in the both settings. The anecdotal evidence suggests because of their impulsivity and inattention-disorganization ADHD offenders are more likely than those without ADHD to

- Have trouble keeping track of appointments and thus fail to appear for court hearings, meet with their attorney, probation or parole officer, appear late, forget items they should bring, etc.
- Change residence without giving notice, neglecting to stay in touch with the court and even their own attorney.
- Procrastinate on retaining an attorney or conditions of release, such as seeking substance abuse treatment or counseling.
- Impulsively fire their attorney for not doing what they want the attorney to do.
- Be non-compliant with basic probationary requirements such as reporting for meetings, keeping a job, attending anger-management classes, paying court-ordered expenses, and undergoing drug, alcohol, or gambling counseling.

Prison Services

This setting also has some research and has yielded two salient findings. First, a meta-analysis of 18 studies with data for 1615 juvenile and adult offenders with ADHD and 3128 without ADHD found an increased risk among ADHD adult offenders for SUD, with prevalence estimates as high as 74% (Young et al., 2015), as would be expected from the previously discussed developmental pathway model. Surprisingly however, there was a lack of association between ADHD and SUD in juvenile offenders which the authors attribute to the low power of the studies to detect potential associations. Second, inmates with ADHD are more likely to engage in disruptive behavior than those without ADHD (Young et al., 2018). As Young (2014, p. 18) observed "Our studies have found that people with ADHD are associated with a greater number of aggressive incidents in prison. These people get into trouble because of their volatility. They struggle to control their behavior in the institutional setting, and therefore lose the opportunity of early release." However, in contrast to these findings, there is anecdotal evidence that some inmates with ADHD actually function better in a prison setting than in the community because the "structure, routine, and predictability of their daily schedule" reduces the likelihood of the occurrence of their ADHD symptoms (Murphy & Appelbaum, 2017, p.4).

Vignette

My friend was sentenced slightly over one week ago and his ADHD medication has not been administered by the county jail despite numerous requests to do so. His hyperactivity is provoking marked anxiety in other inmates and himself, resulting in altercations as he does laps pacing common areas, fidgets uncontrollably, speaks rapidly, and interrupt incessantly. His mind races when it's time to sleep and resorts to exhausting himself with hours of sit ups and push ups in the dark. It took him three days to write a one and a half page dilapidated letter to me. Always perpetually combating boredom, the more unpredictable ins and outs of impulse control have returned vigorously in an unfamiliar social environment on top of the vast psychological stresses involving incarceration itself. It has only been one week.

Author's case

CHAPTER FIVE

IDENTIFICATION

The identification of ADHD in the criminal justice system involves a two-step procedure: screening for ADHD and referral of those who screen positive for a comprehensive evaluation.

Screening

The guidelines for the provision of psychiatric services for inmates in correctional facilities of the American Psychiatric Association (Trestman et al., 2016) recommend that each newly admitted inmate receive an intake mental health screening within 14 days of arrival at a correctional facility. A screening for ADHD should be part of this general mental health screening. Two screening instruments for ADHD are available. The first is the *Adult Attention-Deficit/Hyperactivity Disorder Self-Report Scale* for DSM-5 (Ustun et al., 2017). It consists of 6 items that are easily scored and has been found to detect the vast majority of general population cases with few false positives (i.e., falsely indicating that an individual has ADHD). The scale is available at *https://nyulangone.org/conditions/attention-deficit-hyperactivity-disorder-in-adults/diagnosis#tests*. The only screening tool for ADHD validated on a prison population (to the author's knowledge) has been developed in a study by Young and colleagues (2016). Their study set out to evaluate the *Barkley Adult ADHD Rating Scale* (a self-report instrument) as a screening measure for detecting ADHD cases in a UK prison sample. A sample of 390 adult male inmates were screened using the Barkley scale and interviewed via the *Diagnostic Interview for ADHD in Adults*. The study then proceeded to develop a briefer scale to the maximize the accuracy the scale to detect ADHD as determined by the interview. Using this procedure, the screen had an overall accuracy of 81%. As this screen is only 6 items it is a feasible and acceptable tool to administer and can be downloaded for free from www.psychology-services.uk.com. In addition to the use of one of these instruments, two questions should also be included in the screening (Young et al., 2016). Whether the inmate had ever been diagnosed with ADHD by a doctor or mental health professional and whether the individual had ever received medication for ADHD. This question can be modified to ask if the inmate ever received medication for being *hyper*, as the inmate may not be familiar with the term ADHD.

Evaluation

There are no objective tests (medical, cognitive, brain or neuropsychological) that can provide a simple, accurate way to diagnose ADHD (Arms et al., 2016; Asherson et al., 2016; Barkley, 2015h; Brown, 2017; Hinshaw & Scheffler, 2014; Loo & Arns, 2015; Ramsay, 2015; Thapar & Cooper, 2016). An accurate diagnosis of ADHD, as is the case for virtually all mental disorders, can only be made by the comprehensive gathering and evaluation of various information streams to document symptoms, impairments and onset of the disorder (Faraone et al., 2015). This requires that the evaluation be conducted by a mental health professional with an expertise in ADHD diagnosis (NICE, 2018; Trestman et al., 2016). This expertise is especially required for diagnosing adults in a forensic setting for two reasons. First, diagnosis of adult ADHD in general is particularly challenging since adults may overreport subclinical symptoms, misperceive normative variations in cognition and behavior, or have another mental disorder (e.g., SUD) with overlapping symptoms (Sibley, Coxe, & Molina, 2017; Sibley et al., 2018). In addition, prisoners may purposely feign ADHD in the hope of receiving medication that they can misuse or divert (Appelbaum & Murphy, 2015). Second, these challenges are magnified in a forensic setting as individuals "routinely present with complex histories that may include multiple comorbidities, personality disorders, trauma, longstanding substance use, poverty, head injuries, or major mental illness" that can mimic ADHD (Appelbaum & Murphy, 2015, p. 202).

In gathering the information, the expert should use a well-normed ADHD rating scale and a diagnostic interview format. There are several to choose from (Adler, Shaw, & Alperin, 2015; Silverstein et al., 2018). In addition to using these instruments to obtain information from the offender, it cannot be emphasized enough, as previously discussed, that if at all possible, information should also be gathered from collateral informants. Parents would be especially critical for obtaining information on ADHD symptom/impairment onset as well as possibly being able to provide historical records such as report cards, psychological test reports, special education records, etc. that might otherwise not be available. Once all the information has been gathered, the expert will determine whether the criteria for an ADHD diagnosis have been met. In doing so, the diagnosis should be informed by two recent findings. First, the evaluation should focus on assessing and weighing more heavily the DSM symptoms of inattention-disorganization which have been found to be more developmentally sensitive to the manifestation adult ADHD than the symptoms of hyperactivity-impulsivity (Martel, Nigg, & Schimmack, 2017). The most likely reason for this differential sensitivity is that hyperactive-impulsive symptoms such as “leaves seat,” “plays quietly,” “blurts out,” etc. are more likely to reflect a childhood rather than an adult manifestation of this symptom dimension as compared to the symptoms of inattention-disorganization. Also, the evaluation should rely more on the information provided by collateral informants, as this information is more accurate than that based upon the self-report of the individual being evaluated. Second, with regard to the number of symptoms needed to diagnose ADHD, as previously discussed, research has shown that a cut-off of 4 rather than the 5 symptoms required by DSM-5 has more empirical validity (Roberts et al., 2015). This finding recently received impressive support from what is arguably the best study to date to provide guidelines for diagnosing ADHD in young adults as it involved participants from the landmark MTA study. Sibley and colleagues (2017) found that a norm-based threshold (i.e., a threshold based on the presence of elevated ADHD symptomatology or impairment when compared to control-group norms) of 4 symptoms rather than the 5 required by DSM-5 criteria optimized diagnostic accuracy.

CHAPTER SIX

TREATMENT

The chapter will begin with a discussion of the major findings in the treatment of adult ADHD. It will then discuss the research that has evaluated the effect treatment of ADHD has on reducing criminal behavior. It will conclude with recommendations for the management of ADHD in the criminal justice system.

Treatment of Adult ADHD

As Hinshaw (2018) has noted, the literature on the treatment of ADHD is so vast than an entire review could be devoted to discussing the essential issues. This discussion therefore must of necessity provide a selective overview with a focus on adults. The reader who might be interested in the voluminous literature on the treatment of children with ADHD can consult reviews by Connor (2015), Hinshaw and Arnold (2015), Smith and Shapiro (2015), and Stevens and Wilens (2015). Parenthetically, it should also be noted that the quality of the evidence from more than 300 RCT studies (Prince et al., 2015) supporting the short-term efficacy of stimulant medication (methylphenidate) for children with ADHD has recently been questioned largely on the grounds that the raters of the children's response to the treatment in the studies (parents and clinicians) were not effectively "blinded" (Catala-Lopez et al., 2017; Storebo et al., 2015). That is, because the raters might easily have known which children were taking the medication and which were not because of common adverse side effects of sleep difficulties and appetite reduction, they might have been biased towards overestimating positive treatment effects. However, several aspects of the methodology and interpretation undergirding this criticism have been contested (Banaschewski, et al., 2016; Sayal, Prasad, Daley, Ford, & Coghill, 2018). Most importantly, findings of treatment effectiveness comparable to those reported by parents/clinicians have been found in studies involving ratings by teachers who were unlikely to be aware of the medication's adverse effects and therefore not prone to bias (Banaschewski, et al., 2016; Hoekstra & Buitelaar, 2016). Studies have also found improvements in several domains of cognitive functioning such as memory and response inhibition (Coghill et al., 2014) and normalization of brain structure and functioning which presumably underlies the positive effects on symptoms and cognitive functioning (Friedman & Rapoport; Rubia et al., 2014; Silberstein, Levy, Pipingas, & Farrow, 2017; Spencer et al., 2013). As these studies involve strictly objective criteria, not subjective ratings, bias due to possible ineffective blinding would not seem to be an issue. In short, the findings from numerous studies in which the risk of bias is minimal to non-existent strongly support the validity of the findings of the far more numerous studies based upon parental/clinician report.

For adults with ADHD only two truly evidence-based interventions exist (a) medication, chiefly stimulants but also noradrenergic agents,[1] and (b) cognitive behavioral forms of psychosocial treatment (Hinshaw, 2018).

Medication

With the exception of pre-school age children, stimulants are generally considered to be the first-line treatment for patients of all ages with ADHD (Faraone et al., 2015; NICE, 2018; Prince, Wilens, Spencer & Biederman, 2015; Sayal, Prasad, Daley, Ford, & Coghill, 2018).[2] Hundreds of RCT trials, most of which have been conducted on children, have found moderate to large clinical effects for ADHD symptoms over the short-term, i.e., several weeks to a couple of months (Asherson et al., 2016; Connor, 2015; De Crescenzo, Cortese, Adamo, & Janti, 2017; Faraone et al., 2015; Hinshaw, 2018; Hinshaw & Arnold, 2015; Prince et al., 2015). In general, similar effects are seen in adults (Faraone et al., 20115). Small to moderate effects have also been found for symptoms of emotional dysregulation in adults (Lenzi, Cortese, Harris, & Masi, 2018). Overall, stimulant medications can significantly improve ADHD impairments in about 80% of people, with some experiencing huge improvements (Brown, 2017). Indeed, "Sometimes the effects of stimulants are night and day" (Hinshaw & Scheffler, 2014, p. 181).

There is a paucity of RCT studies for longer term benefits (Asherson et al., 2016; De Crescenzo et al., 2017; Faraone et al., 2015; Prince et al,

---

[1] Appendix 1 provides a list of the medications approved for the treatment of ADHD by the United States Food and Drug Agency.

[2] Although the most recent guidelines (March 14, 2018) from the National Institute for Health and Care and Excellence in the UK recommend that for children medication be considered only after environmental modifications have proven inadequate, for adults stimulants are recommended as the first line treatment (NICE, 2018).

2015). However, the small number of RCT studies when combined with open-label studies (i.e., studies that are not blinded or placebo controlled) have reported beneficial effects for at least 2 years (Faraone et al., 2015). In addition, large population studies using national registry data have found substantial long term benefits for reduction of both ADHD symptoms and serious impairments such as transport accidents, suicidal behavior, substance abuse, and criminal convictions (Asherson et al., 2016). The findings on criminal convictions as well as substance abuse are of critical importance to this book and will subsequently be discussed in detail.

On average, stimulants (amphetamine and methylphenidate) are more efficacious than non-stimulants (atomoxetine, guanfacine, and clonidine) [Asherson et al., 2016; Faraone et al., 2015; Hinshaw, 2018]. Stimulant medications primarily act on the dopamine system by increasing its release and blocking its re-uptake[3] which improves communication both within and between the brain networks involved in ADHD (Brown, 2017; Prince et al., 2015). The efficacy of both classes of stimulants is similar. While some patients respond better to one or the other, there is no reliable way of predicting preferential responsiveness (Faraone et al., 2015). Stimulants are generally well tolerated but do have commonly occurring side effects such as insomnia, decreased appetite, dysphoria, and irritability (Faraone et al., 2015; Prince et al., 2015). These tend to be short-term and usually respond to adjustment in dosage, timing, or use of another stimulant (Brown, 2017).

Serious adverse side effects such as acute anxiety, depression, psychosis and mania are rare and tend to occur in individuals who possess a pre-existing vulnerability (Connor, 2015; Faraone et al., 2015). Previous concerns about increased risk for tics or seizures are unwarranted if adults take the medication as prescribed (Brown, 2017; Cohen et al., 2015; Connor, 2015; Wiggs et al., 2018). For patients with pre-existing heart conditions, stimulants should be used cautiously. In all patients treated with stimulants, blood pressure should be monitored during treatment (Faraone et al., 2015), as stimulants have been found to result in small increases in blood pressure and heart rate which may be clinically significant for a minority of individuals who experience larger increases

---

[3] Nerve cells communicate through chemical messages/signals carried by various neurotransmitters (i.e., brain chemicals) such as dopamine. If the signal is too weak as in ADHD, the communication is impaired. Stimulants can increase the strength of the signal by either increasing the release of the neurotransmitter or by blocking a process that vacuums up (i.e., re-uptake) the neurotransmitter that has been released (Brown, 2017).

(Hennissen et al., 2017). Interactions with prescription or nonprescription medications are generally mild and not a source of concern (Prince et al., 2015).

The following vignette illustrates how stimulants can effect a "night and day" change in functioning. Also recall the previous vignette of "David's Story."

Vignette

I received a diagnosis of ADHD in second grade and was never medicated. As I reached middle school, the symptoms became more and more apparent. I was impulsive, rarely taking the time to consider the consequences of my actions. My grades slipped, and I began to get into serious trouble at school. By the time I was in ninth grade, I was using drugs and alcohol, and a year later I was kicked out of private school. Despite all of this, our family therapist refused to consider stimulant medication as an option. She opted instead for antidepressants and antipsychotics. A stimulant called Adderall turned my life around. At 18, I suddenly found myself able to focus and excel in all my classes. I graduated college cum laude and am now applying to medical school.

Alexander Busko (2012)

Cognitive Behavioral Treatments

Cognitive Behavioral Treatments (CBTs) involve training individuals in cognitive and behavioral skills such as organization, planning, and time management to address ADHD symptoms and associated deficits. (Knouse, 2015; Knouse, Teller, & Brooks, 2017). A meta-analysis of 32 studies of CBT for adult ADHD reported medium to large effects for self-reported symptoms and functioning (Knouse et al., 2017). The effects were not moderated by medication status, nor were they larger for treatments that lasted longer. However, the meta-analysis also found that those studies that used an RCT design showed reduced effects, i.e., small-to-medium effects, and that only two studies used attention-matched control groups. The authors concluded that "…additional tightly controlled studies of CBT for adult ADHD are needed" (Knouse et al., 2017, p. 746). A second meta-analysis which only included RCT studies of CBT for adult ADHD (N=14) reached a similar conclusion (Lopez et al., 2018). It noted however that the evidence for the short-term reduction of core ADHD symptoms and improved global functioning was of low quality. Therefore, since the evidence for the benefit of CBT is less than it is for stimulant medication (NICE, 2018), CBTs are best utilized as a complement or adjunct to stimulant treatment targeting impairments secondary to ADHD rather than the core symptoms (Asherson et al., 2016; Faraone et al., 2015). This is analogous to the role that behavior therapy plays in the treatment of childhood ADHD which has been found to be effective in treating associated conduct problems but not core ADHD symptoms (Daley et al., 2017).

The following vignette illustrates the adjunctive role that CBTs can play in the treatment of ADHD.

Vignette

I think you hit the nail on the head, so to speak. The way I see it in working with adolescents and in my own experience with ADHD, medication treatment is the enabling factor that brings an individual back to more normative functioning, but oftentimes the importance of skills training is minimized in treatment. In my own experience, once the medication started to work for me I really needed training in things like time management, organization, and self-regulation. When I work at the hospital, that is also a large proportion of our programming and intervention work, because most of the children with ADHD and other forms of dysregulated behavior are often very deficient in these domains. In my case, I needed help structuring my life through things such as keeping a date book/notebook and writing things down and keeping a running "check" mark log where I crossed things off. This seems very basic and common sense, but kids who have grown up disorganized and dysregulated need someone to help them add that structure.

Young male adult (author's case)

Treatment for ADHD and Criminality

This is the most important topic of the book. For, if there are studies that provide strong evidence that treatment of ADHD substantially reduces criminal behavior, then the identification of offenders with ADHD and their effective treatment can make a significant contribution to reducing recidivism. To the author's knowledge there are 3 such studies, all involving medication. In addition to these studies, there also are studies of the effectiveness of stimulant treatment of ADHD in reducing the risk of SA. Given the previously discussed strong linkage between SA and criminality, reduction of risk for SA in individuals with ADHD can result in a corresponding reduction in criminality.

Criminality

In the first study, Lichenstein and colleagues (2012), using data from population-based national registers in Sweden, gathered information on 25,656 patients with a diagnosis of ADHD, their pharmacological treatment, and subsequent criminal convictions from 2006 to 2009. They then compared the rate of criminality while the patients were receiving ADHD medications (mostly stimulants) to the rate when the same patients were not receiving medication. As compared to the non-medication periods, there was a significant reduction of 32% in the criminality rate for men and 41% for women when they were on medication. The reductions were the same for less severe and more severe crimes such as assault and homicide as well as substance-related crimes. The study's design enabled the authors to rule out three possible confounds to the interpretation that stimulant medication use caused a reduction in criminality.

First, there was the possibility of *selection bias* in that the patients who selected to receive medication might be different from those who chose not to. This possibility was eliminated because of the study's design in which the crime rates were examined in the same person, not different persons, during medication compared to non-medication periods. Second, there was the possibility of *reverse causation.* Namely, the association between medication use and criminality may have occurred because patients who decided to start taking medication also decided to make other changes in their life, e.g., change criminal behavior. Or, vice versa, patients who decided to stop taking medication did so because of a desire to engage in criminal behavior. Third, there was also the possibility that unmeasured confounders related to the use of prescription drugs, such as engagement with social services that provide prescriptions, rather than the effect of the drugs themselves caused the reduction in criminality. Both of these possibilities were addressed by examining the association between anti-depressant medication and criminality. If reverse causation or confounding occurred, then there should have been a similar association between rates of criminality and periods of using and not using antidepressant medication as occurred with the use of stimulant medication. There was not. Crucially, the evidence for the association between the use of ADHD stimulant medication and crime reduction only occurred when the patients were taking the stimulant medication. There were no long-term reductions in crime rate after termination of the medication. This is exactly what is to be expected since as Brown (2017) points out, taking medication for ADHD is like wearing glasses for vision problems, or one might add, taking insulin for diabetes. The treatments cure nothing. Treatment must be ongoing to be effective. Lastly, since

Sweden does not appear to be unusual in its rates of ADHD, or the use of ADHD medication (Lichtenstein et al., 2012), the findings from the study can probably be generalized to similar cultures. In sum, this very well-designed large population study convincingly demonstrated that the use of stimulant medication can dramatically reduce the risk of criminality among individuals with ADHD.

In the second study, Chang and colleagues (2016a) conducted a longitudinal study of 22,275 released prisoners (92% male) in Sweden from 2005 to 2010 to examine the association between main classes of psychotropic medication and violent reoffending. The median length of the follow-up was 4.6 years and 5.4% of the prisoners were dispensed stimulant medication. There were two main findings. First, three classes of psychotropic medications (stimulants, antipsychotics, and drugs used in addictive disorders) were associated with substantial reductions in violent reoffending. For stimulants, offenders were 43% less likely to commit a violent offence during medication periods compared to non-medication periods. The second major finding was that the magnitudes of the reduction in violent offending associated with psychotropic medication were as strong as, and possibly stronger than those of psychosocial programs that are widely used in prisons.

As in the Lichenstein and colleagues study (2012), the possibility of selection bias, reverse causation, or confounding were addressed and ruled out using the same methodology. Namely, selection bias could not have occurred since the same persons were examined during medication and non-medication periods. Similarly, since other medication classes (antidepressant, anti-epileptics, and adrenergic inhalants) were not associated with any significant differences in violent reoffending rates, reverse causation or confounding by other variables was highly unlikely.
Lastly, the authors pointed out that since exposure to medication using dispensed prescriptions does not account for the common problem of poor medication adherence, it is possible that the reduction in violent offending would have been greater if strict adherence were insured. Moreover, as the findings from the MTA study have shown,[4] it is also possible/likely that if the medication protocol was optimized and also accompanied by cognitive-behavior treatment there would have been a further reduction in

[4] When parent and teacher ratings of ADHD were combined to yield a measure of "excellent response (ER)," the rate of response in the group that received optimal stimulant treatment combined with behavior therapy had an ER of 68% in contrast to the 25% ER of the community group that received typical care (Hinshaw & Arnold, 2015).

criminal offending. These considerations also apply to the Lichenstein and colleagues study (2012).

In contrast to the two prior large population studies, the third study was conducted in a Swedish high-security prison using a small sample of 30 adult male inmates with ADHD who were convicted almost exclusively for violent or drug related offenses (Ginsberg, Langstrom, Larsson, & Lindefors, 2015). The prisoners, who were described as highly motivated, completed a 52 week trial with a stimulant (methylphenidate) beginning with a 5-week RCT trial followed by 47-week open-label extension of the treatment of 25 of the prisoners. This treatment was accompanied by the regular prison-based offender treatment programs within the prison setting. Medication was found to be highly effective for reducing ADHD symptoms, improving global functioning and behavior control both at 5 weeks and at 52 weeks as judged by blinded observers. No misuse of ADHD medication was detected by repeated, mandatory urine toxicology throughout the study period. Fifteen of the offenders were followed-up 3 years after the end of study. Methylphenidate-related improvements in ADHD symptoms (50% reduction from pretrial levels) and psychosocial functioning obtained during the 52-week trial were maintained based upon self-report and a psychiatric evaluation, especially for those who continued medication (10/15). Further, the recidivism rate of 40% based upon self-report was substantially lower than the expected rate of 70-80%. In conclusion, although this study has a very small sample size and lacked an untreated control group, except for the first 5-weeks, it does add to the sparse literature on the efficacy of stimulant treatment for offenders with ADHD in improving functioning and reducing recidivism. Most importantly, it demonstrates that stimulant medication can be highly effective for reducing ADHD symptoms and improving global functioning in a prison setting without misuse of the medication.

Substance Abuse

As previously discussed, the link between SA and criminal offending is one of the most reliable findings in criminology. Given this linkage, it follows that the effective treatment of SA should reduce criminality. For example, Wen, Hockenberry, and Cummings (2014) estimated that a relative 10 percent increase in SA treatment can reduce robbery rate by 3 percent, aggravated assault rate by 4 to 9 percent, and larceny theft rate by 2 to 3 percent. It also follows that if treatment of ADHD reduces risk for SA, there should be a corresponding reduction in risk for criminal behavior. Three studies provide strong support for this logical inference.

The first study to be reviewed examined the association between stimulant treatment for ADHD and reduced risk for SA. Two other studies evaluated the relationship between stimulant treatment for ADHD and reduced risk for SA-related crime.

In the largest study to date using registry data, Quinn and colleagues (2017) analyzed commercial health care claims from 2,993,887 adolescents and adults with ADHD in the United States to evaluate the relationship between pharmacological treatment for ADHD (mostly stimulant treatment) and reduction in SA-related events, such as emergency room visits. The study found that relative to periods in which patients did not receive stimulant treatment, males had a 35% lower risk of concurrent SA-related problems and a 19% lower risk of SA-related events 2 years after medication periods. As previously discussed regarding criminality, the weaker long-term reduction in risk for SA-related problems relative to concurrent reduction might be due the failure to continue treatment with stimulants. The possibility of problems of selection bias, reverse causation, or confounding were addressed and ruled out using the same methodology as in the studies on crime reduction. Namely, selection bias could not have occurred since the same persons were examined during medication and non-medication periods. Similarly, antidepressant medication was, if anything, associated with an *increase* rather than a *decrease* in SA-related events, thereby indicating that reverse causation or confounding by other variables were highly unlikely explanations for the reduction in SA-related events associated with stimulant treatment for ADHD. In addition, Quinn and colleagues (2017) also put forth a second reason for casting doubt on reverse causation or confounding by other variables as plausible alternative explanations. They noted that stimulant treatment of individuals with ADHD has also been associated with a 38% decreased risk of motor vehicle crashes for males (Chang et al. 2017b), a 46% decreased rate of emergency room visits for children (Dalsgaard et al., 2015), and a 49% reduced risk for traumatic brain injury for children and adolescents (Liao et al., 2018). These findings are less susceptible to alternative causal explanations. For, although it is plausible that some life events might prompt an individual with ADHD to simultaneously decrease their SA and seek treatment, it is far less plausible that somehow some life event(s) caused an individual with ADHD to not engage in the type of reckless behavior that could cause car accidents and various forms of injury and simultaneously seek treatment for ADHD. Therefore, if there is almost surely a causal connection between treatment with stimulant medication and substantially reduced accidents and injuries, this supports the high likelihood that there is also a similar causal connection between stimulant treatment for ADHD and substantially reduced SA. This same reasoning also provides additional support for a causal interpretation of an association between stimulant treatment for ADHD and reduction in criminality.

Stimulant treatment of ADHD has also been linked to reduced risk for SA-related crime in two studies. As previously reviewed, Lichtenstein and colleagues (2012) found a reduction in SA-related crime of 32% and 41% for males and females respectively during medication periods. In a second study, Chang and colleagues (2014) using national registry data from Sweden studied 26,249 men and 12,504 women diagnosed with ADHD to investigate the association between treatment of ADHD with stimulant medication and SA over a 3-year period. They found a 31% reduction in SA-related problems such as hospital visits, death, and *crime.* Furthermore, the study found that the longer the duration of treatment, the lower the rate of SA-related problems. Potential problems of selection bias, reverse causation, and confounding variables were rendered highly unlikely for the same reasons as were discussed in the large population studies of stimulant ADHD medication and criminality in Sweden.

Lastly, the reader will recall the discussion in chapter 4 that in order to establish that an association between a risk factor (i.e., ADHD) and an outcome (i.e., criminality) is causal, it must be shown that manipulation of the risk factor changes the outcome. This can be done by removing the risk factor and observing the effect on outcome. This removal can be simulated through studying the effects of treatment on ADHD which in effect reduces/removes ADHD as a risk factor. Such a simulation is seen in the studies of Lichtenstein and colleagues (2012) and Chang and colleagues (2016a) which demonstrated that treatment with stimulant medication substıntially reduces the risk of criminal offending. Furthermore, since criminality increased during non-medication periods, these studies can be viewed as employing an *ABAB* research design typically used to assess the causal effects of treatment for a single individual (Kazdin, 2011). The *ABAB* design examines the effects of a treatment by alternating a condition (A phase) when no treatment is given, with a treatment condition (B phase). The A and B phases are repeated again. If the behavior in the A condition (i.e., criminality) decreases during the B treatment condition with stimulants, increases when treatment is withdrawn (A condition) and once again decreases when treatment is resumed (B condition), this strongly suggests that the treatment was responsible for the change (Kazdin, 2011). This, in effect, is precisely what was found in the Lichtenstein and colleagues (2012) and Chang and colleagues (2016a) studies in that rates of criminality fluctuated between periods of treatment and no treatment. Thus, the final criterion for establishing ADHD as a causal risk factor for criminality is as firmly established as it possibly can be in a studies which observe but don't directly manipulate the putative causal variable.

Vignette

Ben, 32, was a semi-professional on probation for delivery of Schedule 1 controlled substance: cocaine. Ben was working and paying court costs and fines, but he continued to struggle with cocaine abuse. His urinalysis for cocaine came back positive on several occasions, forcing me to send him back for more drug treatment. He was on a beeline back to court for violations of his probation.

In talking with Ben (a very likable guy), I directed the conversation to his past as well as his current situation and frustrations. He wanted to kick the cocaine habit and wanted to be successful on probation. He was struggling with both. At the same time, he wanted to be successful at his sales career but that seemed to take a dip anytime he stopped using cocaine. After several discussions with Ben about the possibility of his having ADHD, he agreed that it seemed he had many of the classic characteristics and we referred him for an evaluation.

Ben phoned me after the evaluations and told me he had learned that he had a substantially above average IQ and that the psychologist thought that he did have ADHD. They were trying to find a medical doctor who might be willing to prescribe him a dose of legal stimulant medication. After some major struggles and writing a letter, we finally got the doctor to write a prescription and I agreed to step up my already intense drug screening of Ben.

Ben made a dramatic turnaround. He never had another positive urinalysis test while on probation. He paid all his court costs and fees and was doing well in his professional and personal life when I last saw him. He was discharged from probation eight months earlier than the original three-year probation term.

Hurley & Eme (2008)

Conclusion

Treatment of ADHD with stimulant medication has been linked to dramatic reductions in SA and criminal behavior as well as substantial reductions for motor vehicle accidents, emergency room visits, and traumatic brain injury. In addition, it has been linked to reduced risk for depression (20%, Chang et al., 2016c) and suicide (18%, Chen et al., 2014). Collectively, these observational studies convincingly indicate that this linkage is causal. Therefore, there is clear, compelling evidence that stimulant treatment of offenders with ADHD can make an important contribution to the reduction of recidivism. Moreover, it is likely that the reduction in recidivism would be even greater if stimulant treatment were optimized and combined with cognitive-behavioral interventions and education about ADHD. Although future research in the form of RCT treatment trials of ADHD in offenders are needed to confirm/replicate the findings of the large scale observational studies, the existing evidence is surely sufficient to make the identification and treatment of the 25% of offenders with ADHD a vital, essential component of mental health services.

Management of ADHD in Correctional and Community Settings

Treatment of ADHD in offenders can occur in either a correctional or community setting. The correctional setting will be addressed first. In the correctional setting, treatment can be expected to have three main benefits (Young et al., 2011). First, the reduction of symptoms that adversely affect behavior (see prior vignette in section on prison services in Chapter 4). Second, the reduction in symptoms, especially those involving impaired attention, should enable individuals to more successfully participate in work, education, and vocational programs. Third, this treatment may lead to improvement in other disorders such as SUD. In contrast to the uncontroversial recommendations of cognitive behavioral interventions and psychoeducation for ADHD, a recommendation for stimulant treatment can be seen as highly problematic. For instance, the high prevalence of comorbid SUD may motivate inmates to report false or exaggerated symptoms to obtain stimulants for abuse or diversion (Applebaum & Murphy, 2015; Trestman et al., 2016). Some inmates may also apply intense pressure to obtain stimulant medication from inmates who nave been appropriately receiving such medication (Trestman et al., 2016). Therefore, this recommendation will require some discussion.

As with any treatment decision for ADHD, the critical criterion is the degree of ADHD-related impairment. And, as previously discussed, some offenders with ADHD might actually function quite well in a prison setting because of its structure and may not need treatment in that setting. Therefore, a diagnosis of ADHD does not automatically warrant treatment. However, given a sufficient level of impairment, stimulant treatment should be considered since it is the first line treatment for adult ADHD. As the task force report on mental health services in correctional facilities of the American Psychiatric Association states "The fundamental policy goal for correctional mental health care is to provide the same quality of mental health services to each patient in the criminal justice system that *should be available* in the community" (Trestman et al., 2016, p. 23). Hence, a decision to restrict access to this standard requires compelling reasons (Applebaum & Murphy, 2015).

One such reason is the previously mentioned risk for misuse/diversion. This risk can be minimized in three ways (Trestman et al., 2016; Young et al., 2011). First, a risk assessment can be conducted in each individual case and only properly motivated inmates should be treated with stimulant medication. One criterion to assess motivation can be the inmate's level of involvement in meaningful activities in the correctional setting. Lack of involvement would contraindicate treatment. Second, since many correctional settings already run medication-based programs for controlled drugs such as methadone maintenance, proper adherence to protocols and policies can reduce the risks of mismanagement. The previously discussed study of inmates in a Swedish high-security prison, many of whom had drug related offenses, demonstrated that treatment could be highly successful without problems of misuse/diversion (Ginsberg et al., 2015). Response to treatment can be monitored through observations from correctional officers, work supervisors, teachers, etc. Third, the use of the long-lasting (10-12 hours) amphetamine-based stimulant *Vyvance* (lisdexamfetamine)[5] can reduce misuse/diversion potential because it is a *prodrug*. A prodrug is a medication that does not become active until it is metabolized in the gastrointestinal tract. Consequently, because it is inactive or significantly less active until conversion to an active drug, this eliminates or reduces the euphoria if abusers change the route of administration by attempting to extract the active drug for injection or insufflation (Gudin & Nalamachu, 2016).

Once the inmate is ready for release into the community, reentry planning should make arrangements with local mental health agencies to continue treatment for ADHD (Trestman et al., 2018). Those inmates with an ADHD diagnosis who did not receive treatment because they did not exhibit any significant impairments in the structured correctional setting should also be referred for treatment since they can be expected to once again exhibit the same ADHD-related impairments that warranted their

[5] This medication along with a methylphenidate-based stimulant (e.g., Ritalin) is the first-line pharmacological treatment for adults with ADHD (NICE, 2018).

diagnosis. As with treatment in correctional facilities, although there are legitimate concerns about misuse/diversion, many professionals who are not well educated about the effectiveness of stimulant treatment for ADHD may become unduly concerned about the abuse potential for simulants (Young et al., 2011), fearing that exposure to stimulants might increase the risk for SA by sensitizing the brain to become more receptive to illicit drugs (Quinn et al., 2017). Two lines of evidence indicate that this concern is unwarranted. First, more than 17 studies have found that childhood treatment of ADHD is not associated with increased risk for SA in adolescence, and a few have found a potentially protective effect if medication was sustained into adolescence (Barkley, 2015f). For example, a recent study using a large nationally representative sample of high school seniors in the U.S. (McCabe, West, & Wilens, 2016) found that stimulant treatment for ADHD was associated with a risk for SA during adolescence that was either lower than or similar to that in the general population if initiated early (aged 9 years or less) and for long duration (6 years or more). Second, and most importantly, the previously discussed research found that stimulant treatment of offenders with ADHD resulted in marked reductions in SA-related crime.

CHAPTER SEVEN

CONCLUSION

ADHD is best conceptualized as a chronic global dysregulation disorder. The vulnerability conferred by this global dysregulation, in interaction with various environmental risk factors, can propel an individual along a pathway of increasingly more severe antisocial behaviors which culminate in criminality. Consequently, approximately 25% of male offenders have ADHD. Since the same quality of mental health services provided to patients in the community should be provided to patients in the criminal justice system, and since stimulants are the first line treatment of ADHD in adults, such treatment should be provided to offenders with ADHD, contingent upon an appropriate evaluation. Such treatment has been found to dramatically reduce recidivism. Furthermore, if stimulant treatment were optimized and combined with cognitive-behavioral treatment as well as education about ADHD for the offender, this remarkable success rate would in all likelihood be even greater. Concerns about stimulant treatment increasing risk for substance abuse related crime are in general unwarranted since, if anything, stimulant treatment has been found to reduce both substance abuse and substance abuse related crime. Although additional research in the form of RCT trials is needed to confirm the findings of large-scale observational population studies on which the success rate is based, the quality of the observational studies is such that a high degree of confidence can be placed in their findings.

In conclusion, to quote a famous criminologist, “It’s elementary.” The identification and treatment of ADHD should be included in the mental health services provided to offenders in correctional and community settings.

REFERENCES

Achenbach, T. (2016). Internalizing/externalizing problems: Review and recommendations for clinical and research application. *Journal of the American Academy of Child and Adolescent Psychiatry, 55,* 645-657.

Adler, L., Faraone, S., Spencer, T., Berglund, P., Alperin, S., & Kessler, R. (2016). The structure of adult ADHD. *International Journal of Methods in Psychiatric Research, 26,* e1555.

Adler, L., Shaw, D., & Alperin, S. (2015). ADHD diagnosis and symptom assessment scales for adults. In L. Adler, T. Spencer, & T. Wilens (Eds.), *Attention-Deficit Hyperactivity Disorder in adults and children* (224-232). Cambridge: Cambridge University Press.

Ahmad, S., & Hinshaw, S. (2016). Attention-Deficit/Hyperactivity Disorder: Similarities to and differences from other externalizing disorders. In T. Beauchaine & S. Hinshaw (Eds.), *The Oxford handbook of externalizing spectrum disorders* (pp. 19-37). New York: Oxford University Press.

American Psychiatric Association. (2013). *Diagnostic and statistical manual of mental disorders* (5th ed.). Washington, DC: Author.

Anderson, V. & Yeates, K. (2014). Children and adolescents. In H. Levin, D. Shum, & C. Chan (Eds.). *Understanding traumatic brain injury: Current research and future directions* (pp. 333-355.). New York: Oxford University Press.

Apel, R., & Horney, J. (2017). How and why does work matter? Employment conditions, routine, activities, and and crime among adult male offenders. *Criminology, 55,* 307-343.

Appelbaum, K., & Murphy, K. (2015). Attention deficit disorders. In K. Trestman, K. Appelbaum, & J. Metzner (Eds.), *Oxford textbook of correctional psychiatry* (pp. 200-204). New York: Oxford University Press.

Arciniegas, D., & Wortzel, H. (2014). Emotional and behavioral dyscontrol after traumatic brain injury. *Psychiatric Clinics of North America, 37,* 31-53.

Arms, M., Loo, S., Sterman, M., Heinrich, H., Kuntsi, J., Asherson, P., Banaschewski, T., & Brandeis, D. (2016). Editorial perspective: How should child psychologists and psychiatrists interpret FDA approval?

Caveat emptor. *Journal of Clinical Child and Adolescent Psychiatry, 57,* 656-658.

Asherson, P. (2017). Drug treatments for ADHD reduce risk of substance use disorders. *American Journal of Psychiatry, 174,* 827-828.

Asherson, P., Buitelaar, J., Faraone, S., & Rohde, L. (2016). Adult attention-deficit hyperactivity disorder: key conceptual issues. *Lancet Psychiatry, 3,* 568-578.

Baddeley, A. (2012). Working memory: Theories, models and controversies. *Annual review of Psychology, 63,* 12.1-12.29.

Banaschewski, T., Buitelaar, J., Chui, C., Coghill, D., Cortese, S., Simonoff, E., & Wong, I. (2016). Methylphenidate for ADHD in children and adolescents: Throwing the baby out with the bath water. *Evidence Based Mental Health, 19,* 97-99.

Barkley, R. (2011). *Barkley Adult ADHD Rating Scale-IV*. New York: Guilford Press.

—. (2015a). *Attention-deficit hyperactivity disorder: A handbook for diagnosis & treatment* (4th ed.). New York: Guilford Press.

—. (2015b). Concentration deficit disorder. In R. Barkley (Ed.), *Attention-deficit hyperactivity disorder*, (4th ed., pp. 435-454). New York: Guilford Press.

—. (2015c). Emotional dysregulation is a core component of ADHD. In R. Barkley (Ed.), *Attention-deficit hyperactivity disorder*, (4th ed., pp. 81-115). New York: Guilford Press.

—. (2015d). Executive functioning and self-regulation viewed as an extended phenotype: Implications of the theory for ADHD and its treatment. In R. Barkley (Ed.), *Attention-deficit hyperactivity disorder*, (4th ed., pp. 405-434). New York: Guilford Press.

—. (2015e). Etiologies of ADHD. In R. Barkley (Ed.), *Attention-deficit hyperactivity disorder*, (4th ed., pp. 356-390). New York: Guilford Press.

—. (2015f). Health problems and related impairments in children and adults with ADHD. In R. Barkley (Ed.), *Attention-deficit hyperactivity disorder*, (4th ed., pp. 267-313). New York: Guilford Press.

—. (2015g). Educational, occupational, dating, marital, and financial impairments. In R. Barkley (Ed.), *Attention-deficit hyperactivity disorder*, (4th ed., pp. 314-342). New York: Guilford Press.

—. (2015h). Psychological assessment of children with ADJHD. In R. Barkley (Ed.), *Attention-deficit hyperactivity disorder*, (4th ed., pp. 455-474). New York: Guilford Press.

—. (2016a). Recent longitudinal studies of childhood Attention-deficit hyperactivity disorder: Important themes and questions for further research. *Journal of Abnormal Psychology, 125,* 248-255.

—. (2016b). Emotional dysregulation is a core component of ADHD. *The ADHD Report, 24,* 7-9.

—. (2016c). Is there an adult onset type of ADHD? Issues in establishing persistence and remission of ADHD from childhood to adulthood. *The ADHD Report, 24,* 6-9.

—. (2017). Questions and answers. *The ADHD Report, 25,* 8-9.

Barkley, R., Murphy, K., & Fischer, M. (2008). *ADHD in adults*. New York: Guilford Press.

Beauchaine, T. (2015). Future directions in emotion dysregulation and youth psychopathology. *Journal of Clinical Child and Adolescent Psychology, 44,* 875-896.

Beauchaine, T. & Hinshaw, S. (2016). *The Oxford handbook of externalizing spectrum disorders*. New York: Oxford University Press.

Beauchaine, T., Gatzke-Kopp, L., & Gizer, I. (2017). Genetic, environmental, and epigenetic influences on behavior. In T. Beauchaine & S. Hinshaw (Eds.), *Child and adolescent psychopathology* (3rd ed., 68-109). New York: John Wiley & Sons.

Beauchaine, T. & Klein, D. (2017). Classifying psychopathology: The DSM, empirically based taxonomies, and the research domain criteria. In T. Beauchaine & S. Hinshaw (Eds.), *Child and adolescent psychopathology* (3rd ed., 33-67). New York: John Wiley & Sons.

Beauchaine, T., & McNulty, T. (2013). Comorbidities and continuities as ontogenic processes: towards a developmental spectrum model of externalizing psychopathology. *Development and Psychopathology, 25,* 1505-1527.

Beauchaine, T., Shader, T., & Hinshaw, S. (2016). An ontogenic processes model of externalizing psychopathology. In T. Beauchaine & S. Hinshaw (Eds.), *The Oxford handbook of externalizing spectrum disorders* (485-502). New York: Oxford University Press.

Beauchaine, T., Zisner, A., & Sauder, C. (2017). Trait impulsivity and the externalizing spectrum. *Annual Review of Clinical Psychology, 13,* 343-368.

Becker, D. (2017). "For some reason I find it hard to work quickly": Introduction to the special issue on sluggish cognitive tempo. *Journal of Attention Disorders, 21,* 615-622.

Becker, D., Leopold, D., Burns, G., Jarrett, M., Langberg, J., Marshall, S., …Willcutt, G. (2016). The internal, external, and diagnostic validity of sluggish cognitive tempo: A meta-analysis and critical review. *Journal of the American Academy of Child and Adolescent Psychiatry, 55,* 163-178.

Bhat, V., Joober, R., & Sengupta, S. (2017). New environmental factors can get under the skin: Epigenetics in Attention-Deficit/Hyperactivity Disorder. *Journal of the American Academy of Child and Adolescent Psychiatry, 56,* 278-280.

Blennow, K., Brody, D., Kochanek, P., Levin, H., McKee, A., Ribbers, G., Yaffe, K., … Zettenberg H. (2016). Traumatic brain injuries. *Nature Reviews: Disease Primers, 2,* 1-20.

Braga, T., Cunha, O., & Maia, A. (2018). The enduring effect of maltreatment on antisocial behavior: A meta-analysis of longitudinal studies. *Aggression and Violent Behavior, 40,* 91-100.

Brown, S., Tomlinson, K., & Winward, J. (2017). Substance use disorders. In T. Beauchaine & S. Hinshaw (Eds.), *Child and adolescent psychopathology* (3rd ed., 497-528). New York: John Wiley & Sons.

Brown, T. (2013). *A new understanding of ADHD in children and adults.* New York: Routledge.

—. (2017). *Outside the box: Rethinking ADD/ADHD in children and adults.* American Psychiatric Publishing: Arlington, VA.

Burke, J., Rowe, R., Stepp, S., Hipwell, A., Boylan, K., Duku, E., & Waldman, I. (2014). Identifying the irritability dimension of ODD: Applications of a modified bifactor model across five large community samples of children. *Journal of Abnormal Psychology, 123,* 841-851.

Burke, J., Waldman, I., & Lahey, B. (2010). Predictive validity of childhood oppositional defiant disorder and conduct disorder: Implications for the DSM-V. *Journal of Abnormal Psychology, 119,* 739-751.

Bushway, S. (2013). Life-course-persistent offenders. In F. Cullen & P. Wilcox (Eds.), *Oxford handbook of criminological theory* (pp. 189-204). New York: Oxford University Press.

Busko, A. (2012). Sunday monologue: Medicating for ADHD. *New York Times,* 12/8/2012 SR BW 2.

Carbonneau, R., Boiven, M., Brendgen, M., Nagin, D., & Tremblay, R. (2016). Comorbid development of disruptive behaviors from age 1½ to 5 years in a population birth-cohort and association with school adjustment in first grade. *Journal of Abnormal Child Psychology, 44,* 677-690.

Carlen, M. What constitutes the prefrontal cortex? *Science, 358,* 478-482.

Castellanos, F., & Aoki, Y. (2016). Intrinsic functional connectivity in Attention-Deficit/Hyperactivity Disorder: A science in development.

Biological Psychiatry: Cognitive Neuroscience and Neuroimaging, 1, 253-261.

Castellanos-Ryan, N., & Sequin, J. (2016). Prefrontal and anterior cingulate cortex mechanisms of impulsivity. In T. Beauchaine & S. Hinshaw (Eds.), *The Oxford handbook of externalizing spectrum disorders* (201-219). New York: Oxford University Press.

Catala-Lopez, F., Hutton, B., Nunez-Beltran, A., Page, M., Rideo, M., Saint-Gerons, D., … Moher, D. (2017). The pharmacological and non-pharmacological treatment of attention deficit hyperactivity disorder in children and adolescents: A systematic review with network meta-analyses of randomized trials. *PLoS One, 12,* e0180355.

Caye, A., Swanson, J., Thapar, A., Sibley, M., Arseneault, L., Hechtman, L., Arnold, L., …Rohde, L. (2016). Life span studies of ADHD-Conceptual challenges and predictors of persistence and outcome. *Current Psychiatry Reports, 19,* 106.

Chang, Z., Lichtenstein, P., Halldner, L., D'Onofrio, B., Seriachius, S., Fazel, S., Langstrom, N., & Larsson, H. (2014). Stimulant ADHD medication and risk of substance abuse. *Journal of Child Psychology and Psychiatry, 55,* 878-885.

Chang, Z., Lichtenstein, P., Langstrom, N., Larsson, H., & Fazel, S. (2016a). Association between prescription of major psychotropic medications and violent reoffending after prison release. *JAMA, 316,* 1798-1807.

Chang, Z., Quinn, P., Hur, K., Gibbons, R., Sjolander, A., Larsson, H., & D'Onofrio, B. (2016b). Association between medication use for Attention-Deficit/Hyperactivity Disorder and risk of motor vehicle accidents. *JAMA Psychiatry, 316,* 319-325.

Chang, Z., D'Onofrio, B., Quinn, P., Lichtenstein, P., & Larsson, H. (2016c). Medication for Attention-Deficit/Hyperactivity Disorder and risk for depression: A nationwide longitudinal study. *Biological Psychiatry, 80,* 912-922.

Chen, Q., Brikell, I., Lichtenstein, P., Serlachius, E., Kuja-Halkola, R., Sandin, S. & Larsson, H. (2017). Family aggregation of attention-deficit/hyperactivity disorder. *Journal of Child Psychology and Psychiatry, 58,* 231-239.

Chen, Q., Sjolander, A., Runeson, B., D'Onofrio, B., Lichtenstein, P., & Larsson, P. (2014). Drug treatment for attention deficit hyperactivity disorder and suicidal behavior: register based study. *BMJ, 348.*

Chien, W., Chung, C., Lin, F., Yeh, C., Huang, S., Lu., R., Chang, H., … Tzeng, N. (2017). The risk of injury in adults with attention-deficit hyperactivity disorder: A nationwide, matched cohort, population-based study in Taiwan. *Research in Developmental Disabilities, 65,* 57-73.

Clark, L., Cuthbert, B., Lewis-Fernandez, R., Narrow, W., & Reed, G. (2017). Three approaches to understanding and classifying mental disorders: *ICD-11, DSM-5,* and the National Institute of Mental Health's Research Domain Criteria (RDoC). *Psychological Science in the Public Interest, 18,* 72-145.

Cohen, S., Mulqueen, S., Ferrancioli-Oda, E., Stuckelman, Z. Coughlin, C., Leckman, J., & Bloch, M. (2015).Meta-analysis: Risk of tics-associated with psychostimulant use in randomized placebo-controlled trials. *Journal of the American Academy of Child and Adolescent Psychiatry, 54,* 728-736.

Coghill, D., Seth, S., Pedroso, S., Usala, T., Currie, J., & Gagliano, A. (2014). Effects of methylphenidate on cognitive functions in children and adolescents with Attention-Deficit/Hyperactivity Disorder: Evidence from a systematic review and meta-analysis. *Biological Psychiatry, 76,* 603-615.

Coker, T., Elliot, M., Toomey, S., Schwebel, D., Cuccaro, P., Emery, S., Davies, S., … Schuster, M. (2016). Racial and ethnic disparities in ADHD diagnosis and treatment. *Pediatrics, 138,* 1-11.

Compas, B. & Andreotti, C. (2013). Risk and resilience is child and adolescent psychopathology. In T. Beauchaine & S. Hinshaw (Eds.), *Child and adolescent psychopathology* (2nd ed., pp. 143-170). Hoboken NJ: Wiley.

Compas, B., Gruhn, M., & Bettis, A. (2017). Risk and resilience in adolescent psychopathology. In T. Beauchaine & S. Hinshaw (Eds.), *Child and adolescent psychopathology* (3rd ed., 113-143). New York: John Wiley & Sons.

Connor, D. (2015). Stimulant and nonstimulant medications for childhood ADHD. In R. Barkley (Ed.), *Attention-deficit hyperactivity disorder*, (4th ed., pp. 666-685). New York: Guilford Press.

Connors, K. (2008). *Connors 3rd*. Toronto ON: Multi-Health Systems.

Cordova, T. & Wilson, M. (2017). Abandoned in their neighborhoods: *Youth joblessness amidst of the flight of industry and opportunity.* Chicago, IL: University of Illinois in Chicago.

Cortese, S. (2016). The genetics of Attention-Deficit/Hyperactivity Disorder: Failure or a learning process? *Journal of the American Academy of Child and Adolescent Psychiatry, 55,* 839-840.

Cradit, T. (2017, October 13, 2017). Fighting the fog. *LD on line.* http://www.ldonline.org/firstperson/Fighting_The_Fog.

Cross, C., Copping, L., & Campbell, A. (2011). Sex differences in impulsivity: A meta-analysis. *Psychological Bulletin, 137*, 97-130.

Curry, A., Metzger, K., Pfeffier, M., Elliott, M., Winston, F., & Power, T. (2017). Motor vehicle crash risk among adolescents and young adult with Attention-Deficit/Hyperactivity Disorder. *JAMA Pediatrics, 17,* 756-763.

Daley, D., Van Der Oord, S., Ferrin, M., Cortese, S., Danckaerts, M., Van den Hoofdakker, B., Coghill, D., … Sonuga-Barke, E. (2017). Practitioner review: Current best practices in the use of parent training and other behavioral interventions in the treatment of children and adolescents with attention-deficit/hyperactivity disorder. *Journal of Child Psychology and Psychiatry,* Advance on line publication 10/30/17

Dalley, J., & Robbins, T. (2017). Fractionating impulsivity: neuropsychiatric implications. *Nature Reviews of Neuroscience, 18,* 158-171.

Dalsgaard, S., Ostergaard, S., Leckman, J., Mortensen, P., & Pedersen, M. (2015). Mortality in children, adolescents and adults with attention-deficit/hyperactivity disorder: a nationwide cohort study. *Lancet, 385,* 2190-2015.

Damasio, A. (1994). *Descartes' error: Emotion, reason, and the human brain.* New York: Grosset/Putnam.

Danforth, J., Connor, D., & Doerfler, 2016). The development of cormorbid conduct problems in children with ADHD: An example of an integrative developmental psychopathology perspective. *Journal of Attention Disorders, 20,* 214-229.

Danielson, M., Bitsko, R., Ghandour, R., Holbrook, J., Kogan, M., & Blumberg, S. (2018). Prevalence of parent-reported ADHD diagnosis and associated treatment among U.S. children and adolescents, 2016. *Journal of Clinical Child and Adolescent Psychology, 47,* 199-212.

De Crescenzo, F., Cortese, S., Adamo, N., & Janin, L. (2017). Pharmacological and non-pharmacological treatment in adults with ADHD: A meta-analysis. *Evidence Based Mental Health, 20,* 4-11.

DeLisi, M. (2011). Self-control theory: The Tyrannosaurus rex of criminology is poised to devour criminal justice. *Journal of Criminal Justice, 39,* 103-105.

DeLisi, M., & Piquero, A. (2011). New frontiers in criminal career research 2000-2011: A state-of-the-art review. *Journal of Criminal Justice, 39,* 289-301.

DeLisi, M., & Vaughn, M. (2014). Foundation for a temperament-based theory of antisocial behavior and criminal justice system involvement. *Journal of Criminal Justice, 42,* 10-25.

DeLisi, M., & Vaugh, M. (2016). Correlates of crime. In A. Piquero (Ed.), *The handbook of criminological theory* (pp. 18-36). New York: John Wiley & Sons.

Demontis, D., Walters, R., Martin, J., Mattheisen, M., Als, T., Agerbo, E., Belliveau, R., … Neale, B. (2017). Discovery of the first genomic-wide significant risk loci for ADHD. *bioRxiv, 14558*, 1-43

Diamond, A. (2013). Executive functions. *Annual review of psychology, 64,* 135-164.

Dishion, T., Kim, H., & Tein, J. (2016). In T. Beauchaine & S. Hinshaw (Eds.), *The Oxford handbook of externalizing spectrum disorders* (pp. 303-312). New York: Oxford University Press.

Dixon, M., Todd, R., Thiruchselvam, R., & Kristoff, K. (2017). Emotion and the prefrontal cortex: An integrative review. *Psychological Bulletin, 143,* 1033-1081.

Doshi, J., Hodgkins, P., Kahle, J., Pharm, V., Cangelos, M., Pharm, J., …Neumann, P. (2012). Economic impact of childhood and adult attention-deficit/hyperactivity disorder in the United States. *Journal of the American Academy of Child and Adolescent Psychiatry, 51*, 990-1002.

DuPaul, G., & Landberg, J. (2015). Educational impairments in children with ADHD. In R. Barkley (Ed.), *Attention-deficit hyperactivity disorder*, (4th ed., pp. 169-190). New York: Guilford Press.

Durose, M., Cooper, A., & Howard, N. (2014). Recidivism of prisoners released in 30 states in 2005: Patterns from 2005 to 2010. *Bureau of Justice Statistics Special Report, April,* NCJ 244205.

Eiden, R., Lessard, J., Colder, C. Livingston, J., Casey, M., & Leonard, K. (2016). Developmental cascade model for adolescent substance use from infancy to late adolescence. *Developmental Psychology, 52*, 1619-1633.

Eisner, M., & Malti, T. (2015). Aggressive and violent behavior. In M. Lamb & R. Lerner (Eds.), *Handbook of child psychology and developmental science,* (7th ed., vol. 3, pp. 795-841). New York: Wiley.

Eme, R. (2015). Pediatric traumatic brain injury and Attention Deficit Hyperactivity Disorder. *The ADHD Report, 23*, 1-8.

Eme, R., & Young, S. (2017). Reliability of ADHD in prison populations. A response to Murphy and Appelbaum. *The ADHD Report, 25,* 1-6.

Engle, R. (2018). Working memory and executive attention: A revisit. *Perspectives on Psychological Science, 13,* 190-193.

Erskine, H., Norman, R., Ferrari, A., Chan, G., Copeland, W., Whitehead, H., & Scott, J. (2016). Long-term outcomes of Attention-Deficit/ Hyperactivity Disorder and conduct disorder: A systematic review and meta-analysis. *Journal of the American Academy of Child and Adolescent Psychiatry, 55,* 841-850.

Fairchild, G., Van Goozen, S., Calder, A., & Goodyer, I. (2013). Research review: Evaluating and reformulating the developmental taxonomic theory of antisocial behaviour. *Journal of Child Psychology and Psychiatry, 54,* 924-940.

Faraone, S., Asherson, P., Banashewski, E., Biederman, J., Buitelarr, J., Ramos-Quiroga, J,. Franke, B. (2015). Attention-Deficit/hyperactivity Disorder. *Nature Review Disease Primers, 1,* 1-23.

Faraone, S., & Biederman, J. (2016). Can attention-deficit/hyperactivity disorder onset occur in adulthood? *JAMA Psychiatry, 73,* 655-656.

Faraone, S., & Larsson, H. (2018). Genetics of attention deficit hyperactivity disorder. *Molecular Psychiatry,* Advance on line publication, 6/11/18.

Farrington, D. (2012). Predictors of young violent offenders. In D. Bishop & B. Feld (Eds.), *The Oxford handbook of juvenile crime and juvenile justice* (pp. 146-174). New York: Oxford University Press.

Farrington, D., & Loeber, R. (2012). Two approaches to developmental life-course theorizing. In F. Cullen & P. Wilcox (Eds.), *Oxford handbook of criminological theory* (pp. 226-256). New York: Oxford University Press.

Fox, J. (2017). Gender differences in patterns and trends in U.S. homicide, 1976-2015. *Violence and Gender, 4,* 1-7.

Franz, A., Bolate, G., Bolat, H., Matijasevach, A., Santos, I., Silviera, R., Procianoy, R., … Moreira-Maja, C. (2018). Attention-deficit/ Hyperactivity Disorder and very preterm/very low birth weight: A meta-analysis *Pediatrics, 141,* e20171645.

Frick, P., Ray, J., Thornton, L., & Kahn, R. (2014). Annual research review: A developmental psychopathology approach to understanding callous-unemotional traits in children and adolescents with serious conduct problems. *Journal of Child Psychology and Psychiatry, 55,* 532-548.

Friedman, L., & Rapoport, J. (2016). Brain development in ADHD. *Current Opinion in Neurobiology, 30,* 106-111.

Gallo, E., & Posner, J. (2016). Moving towards causality in attention-deficit hyperactivity disorder. *Lancet Psychiatry, 3,* 555-567.

Garofalo, C., & Wright, A. (2017). Alcohol abuse, personality disorders, and aggression: The quest for an underlying mechanism. *Aggression and Violent Behavior, 34,* 1-8.

Gerring, J. & Vasa, R. (2016). Head injury and externalizing behavior. In T. Beauchaine & S. Hinshaw (Eds.), *The Oxford handbook of externalizing spectrum disorders* (403-415). New York: Oxford University Press.

Ginsberg, Y., Langstrom, N., Larsson, H., & Lindefors, N. (2015). Long-term treatment outcomes in adult male prisoners with Attention-Deficit/Hyperactivity Disorder. *Journal of Clinical Psychopharmacology, 35,* 535-543.

Gizer, I., Otto, J., & Ellingson, J. (2016). Molecular genetic approaches to studying the externalizing spectrum. In T. Beauchaine & S. Hinshaw (Eds.), *Child and adolescent psychopathology* (3rd ed., 125-169). New York: John Wiley & Sons.

Gormley, M., DuPaul, G., Weyandt, L., & Anastopolous, A., (2016). First-year GPA and academic service use among college students with and without ADHD. *Journal of Attention Disorders,* Advance online publication, 1/7/16

Graziano,P., & Garcia, P. (2016). Attention-deficit/Hyperactivity Disorder and children's emotion dysregulation: A meta-analysis. *Clinical Psychology Review, 46,* 106-123.

Gudin, J., & Nalamachu, S. (2016). An overview of prodrug technology and its application for developing abuse-deterrent opioids. *Postgraduate Medicine, 128,* 97-105.

Gudjonsson, G., Sigurdsson, J., Bragason, O., Newton, A., & Einarsson, E. (2008). Interrogative suggestibility, compliance, and false confessions among prisoners and their relationship with attention deficit hyperactivity disorder (ADHD) symptoms. *Psychological Medicine, 38,* 1037-1044.

Gudjonsson, G., Sigurdsson, J., Bragason, O., Newton, A., & Einarsson, E. (2010). Inattention, hyperactivity/impulsivity and antisocial personality disorder: which is the best predictor of false confessions? *Personality and Individual Differences, 48,* 720-724.

Guelzow, B. Loya, F., & Hinshaw, S. (2017). How persistent is ADHD into adulthood? Informant report and diagnostic thresholds in a female sample. *Journal of Abnormal Child Psychology, 45,* 301-312.

Hallowell, E., & Ratey, J. (2005). *Delivered from distraction.* New York: Ballantine Books.

Hayden, E., & Mash, E. (2014). Child psychopathology: A developmental perspective. In E. Mash & R. Barkley (Eds.), *Child psychopathology* (3rd ed., pp. 3-74). New York: Guilford Press.

Hechtman L. (2017). *Attention Deficit Hyperactivity Disorder: Adult outcome and its predictors.* Oxford University Press.

Hennissen, L., Bakker, M., Banaschewski, T., Carucci, S., Coghill, D., Danckaerts, M., Dittmann, R., … Buitelaar, J. (2017). Cardiovascular effects of stimulant and non-stimulant medication for children and adolescents with ADHD: A systematic review and meta-analysis of trials of methylphenidate, amphetamines and atomoxetine. *CNS Drugs, 31,* 199-215.

Herzhoff, K., & Tackett, J. (2016). Subfactors of oppositional defiant disorder: converging evidence from structural and latent-class analyses. *Journal of Child Psychology and Psychiatry, 57,* 18-29.

Hinshaw, S. (2017). Developmental psychopathology as a scientific discipline: A 21st-century perspective. In T. Beauchaine & S. Hinshaw (Eds.), *Child and adolescent psychopathology* (3rd ed., 3-32). New York: John Wiley & Sons.

Hinshaw, S. (2018). Attention Deficit Hyperactivity Disorder (ADHD): Controversy, developmental mechanisms, and multiple levels of analysis. *Annual review of clinical psychology, 14,* 291-316.

Hinshaw, S., & Arnold, E. (2015). ADHD multimodal treatment, and longitudinal outcomes: Evidence, paradox, and challenge. *Wiley Interdisciplinary Reviews of Cognitive Science, 6,* 39-52.

Hinshaw, S., & Ellison, K. (2016). *ADHD: What everyone needs to know.* New York: Oxford University Press.

Hoekstra, P., & Buitelaar, J. (2016). Is the evidence base of methylphenidate for children and adolescents with attention-deficit/hyperactivity disorder flawed? *European Child and Adolescent Psychiatry, 25,* 339-340.

Hoogman, M., Bralten, J., Hibar, D., Mennes, M., Zwiers, M., Schweren, L., van Hulzen, K., … Kohls, G. (2017). Subcortical brain volume differences in participants with attention-deficit hyperactivity disorder in children and adults: a cross-sectional mega-analysis. *The Lancet Psychiatry, 4,* 310-319.

Housais, S. Hechtman, L., & Klein, R. (2017). Long-term outcomes of childhood Attention Deficit/Hyperactivity Disorder. In. L. Hechtman (Ed.), *Attention Deficit Hyperactivity Disorder: Adult outcome and its predictors* (31-62). New York: Oxford University Press.

Jacobson, L., Crocetti, D., Dirilikov, K., Denckla, M., Mostofsky, S., & Mahone, E. (2018). Anomalous brain development is evident in preschoolers with Attention-Deficit/Hyperactivity Disorder. *Journal of the International Neuropsychological Society, 24,* 1-9.

Jaffee, S. (2017). Child maltreatment and risk for psychopathology in childhood and adulthood. *Annual review of clinical psychology, 13,* 52-551.

Jaffee, S., Strait, L., & Odgers, C. (2012). From correlates to causes: Can quasi-experimental studies and statistical innovations bring us closer to identifying the causes of antisocial behavior? *Psychological Bulletin, 138,* 272-295.

Jennings, W., Perez, N., & Gonzalez, R. (2018). Conduct disorder and neighborhood effects. *Annual review of clinical psychology, 14,* 317-341.

Johnston, C., & Chronis-Tuscano, A. (2015). Families and ADHD. In R. Barkley (Ed.), *Attention-deficit hyperactivity disorder*, (4th ed., pp. 191-209). New York: Guilford Press.

Karalunas, S., Fair, D., Musser, E., Aykes, K., Iyer, S., & Nigg, J. (2014). Subtyping Attention-Deficit/Hyperactivity Disorder using temperament dimensions: Toward biologically based nosologic criteria. *JAMA Psychiatry, 71,* 1015-1024.

Kazdin, A. (2011). *Single-case research designs (2nd ed.)*. New York: Oxford University Press.

Kennedy, M., Kreppner, J., Knights, N., Kumsta, R., Maughan, B., Golm, D., Rutter, M., …Sonuga-Barke, S. (2016). Early severe institutional deprivation is associated with a persistent variant of adult attention-deficit/hyperactivity disorder: clinical presentations, developmental continuities and life circumstances of the English and Romanian Adoptees study. *Journal of Child Psychology and Psychiatry, 57,* 1113-1125.

Kessler, R., Adler, L., Barkley, R., Biederman, J., Connors, K.,…Howes, M. (2006). The prevalence and correlates of adult ADHD in the United States: Results from the National Comorbidity Survey Replication. *The American Journal of Psychiatry, 163,* 716-723.

Kimonis, E., Frick, P., & McMahon, R. (2014). Conduct and oppositional defiant disorders. In E. Mash & R. Barkley (Eds.), *Child psychopathology* (3rd ed., pp. 145-179). New York: Guilford Press.

Knopik, V., Neiderhiser, J., DeFries, J., & Plomin, R. (2017). *Behavioral genetics* (7th ed.). New York: Worth Publishers.

Knouse, L., Teller, J., & Brooks, M. (2017). Meta-analysis of cognitive-behavioral treatments for adult ADHD. *Journal of Consulting and Clinical Psychology, 85,* 737-750.

Lahey, B., Lee, S., Sibley, M., Applegate, B., Molina, B., & Pelham, W. (2016). Predictors of adolescent outcomes among 4-6-year-old children with Attention-Deficit/Hyperactivity Disorder. *Journal of Abnormal Psychology, 125,* 168–181.

Lecendreux, M., Konofal, E., Cortese, S., & Faraone, S. (2015). A four follow-up of attention-deficit/hyperactivity disorder. *Journal of Clinical Psychiatry, 76,* 712-719.

Lee, S., Sibley, M., & Epstein, J. (2016). Attention-Deficit/Hyperactivity Disorder across development: Predictors, resilience, and future directions. *Journal of Abnormal Psychology, 125,* 151-153.

Lenzi, F., Cortese, S., Harris, J., & Masi, G. (2018). Pharmacotherapy of emotional dysregulation in adults with ADHD: A systematic review and meta-analysis. *Neuroscience and Biobehavioral Reviews, 34,* 359-367.

Levy, F. (2007). Pharmcogenomics versus aetiology in ADHD. *The ADHD Report, 15,* 5-8.

Liao, Y., Yang, Y., Kuo, Y., Liang, H., Huang, K., Wang, T., Lee, Y., …Chen, V. (2018). Dosage of methylphenidate and traumatic brain injury in ADHD: A population-based study in Taiwan. *European Child and Adolescent Psychiatry, 27,* 279-288.

Lichtenstein P, Halldner L, Zetterqvist J, Sjolander A, Serlachius E, Fazel S, Langstrom N, & Larsson H. (2012). Medication for attention deficit-hyperactivity disorder and criminality. *The New England journal of medicine*, *367,* 2006-2014.

Loeber R., Burke, J., & Pardini, D. (2009). Perspectives on oppositional defiant disorder, conduct disorder, and psychopathic features. *Journal of Child Psychology and Psychiatry, 50*, 133-142.

Loo, S., & Arns, M. (2015). Should the EEG-based theta to beta ratio be used to diagnose ADHD? *ADHD Report, 23,* 8-13.

Lopez, P., Torrente, F., Ciapponi, A., Lischinsky, A. Cetkovich-Bakmas, M., Rojas, J., Romano, M., & Manes, F. (2018). Cognitive-behavioral interventions for attention-deficit hyperactivity disorder (ADHD) in adults (Review). *Cochrane Database of Systematic Reviews, 5,* No: CD010840.

Lugo-Candelas, C., & Posner, J. (2017) Collective analytics: Advancing the neuroscience of ADHD. *Lancet Psychiatry, 4,* 266-268.

Lykken, D., McGue, M., Tellegen, A., & Bouchard, T. (1992). Emergenesis: Genetic traits that may not run in families. *American Psychologist, 47,* 1565-1577.

MacDonald, A., Goines, K., Novacek, D., & Walker, E. (2016). Prefrontal mechanisms of cormorbidity from a transdiagnostic ontogenic perspective. *Development and Psychopathology, 28,* 1147-1185.

Mannuzza, S., Klein, R., & Moulton, J. (2008). Lifetime criminality among boys with attention deficit hyperactivity disorder: A prospective follow-up study into adulthood using official arrest records. *Psychiatry Research, 160*, 237-246.

Martel, M., Levinson, C., Langer, J., & Nigg, J. (2016). A network analysis of developmental change in ADHD symptom structure from preschool of adulthood. *Clinical Psychological Science, 4,* 988-1004.

Martel, M., Levinson, C., Lee, C., & Smith, T. (2017). Impulsivity symptoms as core to the developmental externalizing spectrum. *Journal of Abnormal Child Psychology, 45,* 83-90.

Martel, M., Nigg, J., & Schimmack, U. (2017). Psychometrically informed approach to integration of multiple informant ratings in adult ADHD in a community-recruited sample. *Assessment, 24,* 279-289.

Max, J. (2014). Neuropsychiatry of pediatric traumatic brain injury. *Psychiatric Clinics of North America, 37*, 125-140.

Mayhew, A., & Meyre, D. (2017). Assessing the heritability of complex traits in humans: Methodological challenges and opportunities. *Current Genomics, 18,* 332-340.

McAllister, T. (2011). Mild brain injury. In J. Silver, T. McAllister, & S. Yudovsky (Eds.), *Textbook of traumatic brain injury* (2nd ed., pp. 239-264). New York: Guilford.

McCabe, S., Dickinson, K., West, B., & Wilens, T. (2016). Age of onset, and type of medication therapy for Attention-Deficit/Hyperactivity Disorder and substance use during adolescence: A multi-cohort national study. *Journal of the American Academy of Child and Adolescent Psychiatry, 55*, 479-486.

McDonough-Caplan, H., & Beauchaine, T. (2018). Conduct disorder: A neurodevelopmental perspective. In M. Martel (Ed.), *Developmental pathways to disruptive, impulse-control, and conduct disorder* (53-89). New York: Elsevier.

McGough J. (2016). New insights from the MTA: Who outgrows Attention-Deficit/Hyperactivity Disorder and what becomes of those who don't? *Journal of the American Academy of Child and Adolescent Psychiatry 55,* 925-926.

McLaughlin, K. (2016). Future directions in child adversity and youth psychopathology. *Journal of Clinical Child and Adolescent Psychology, 45,* 361-382.

McQuade, J., & Hoza, B. (2015). Peer relationships of children with ADHD. In R. Barkley (Ed.), *Attention-deficit hyperactivity disorder*, (4th ed., pp. 210-222.). New York: Guilford Press.

Mitchell, J., Weisner, T., Jensen, P., Murray, D., Molina, B., Arnold, L., Hechtman, L., … Nguyen, J. (2018). How substance users with ADHD perceive the relationship between substance use and emotional functioning. *Journal of Attention Disorders, 22*, 495-605.

McGill, R., & Dombrowski, S. (2017).What school psycholgists need to know about factor analysis. *Communique of National Association of School Psychologists, 46,* 16-18.

Miller, T., Levy, D., Cohen, M., & Cox, K. (2006). Costs of alcohol and drug-involved crime. *Prevention Science, 7*, 333-342.

Moffitt, T. (1993). Life-course-persistent and adolescent-limited antisocial behavior. *Psychology Review, 100,* 893-910.

—. (2005). The new look of behavioral genetics in developmental psychopathology: Gene-environment interplay in antisocial behaviors. *Psychological Bulletin, 131,* 533-554.

—. (2006). Life-course-persistent versus adolescent-limited antisocial behavior. In D. Cicchetti and D. Cohen (Eds.), D*evelopmental psychopathology* (2nd ed., vol. 3, pp. 570 –598). New York: Wiley.

—. (2012). Self-control, then and now. In R. Loeber & B. Welsch (Eds.), *The future of criminology* (pp. 40-45). New York: Oxford University Press.

—. (2018). Male antisocial behavior in adolescence and beyond. *Nature: Human Behaviour, 2,* 177-186.

Moffitt, T., Arseneault, L., Belsky, D., Dickson, N., Hancox, R. Harrington, H., … Caspi, A. (2011). A gradient of childhood self-control predicts health, wealth, and public safety. *Proceedings of the National Academy of Sciences, 108*, 2693-2698.

Moffitt T., Houts R., Asherson P., Belsky D., Corcoran D., Hammerle M., Harrington H., … Caspi A. (2015). Is adult ADHD a childhood-onset neurodevelopmental disorder? Evidence from a four-decade longitudinal cohort study. *American Journal of psychiatry, 172,* 967-977.

Moffitt, T., & Beckley, A. (2015). Abandon twin research? Embrace epigenetic research? Premature advice for criminologists. *Criminology, 53,* 121-126.

Mohr-Jensen, C., Andisen, B., Jorgensen, J., & Arnfrded, S. (2017). Cognitive behavioural therapy for ADHD in adults: Systematic review and meta-analysis. *ADHD Attention Deficit and Hyperactivity Disorders, 8,*3-11.

Molina, B., Howard, A., Swanson, J., Stehli, A., Mitchell, J., Kennedy,T., Epstein, J., … Hoza, B. (2018). Substance use through adolescence into early adulthood after childhood-diagnosed ADHD: Finding from the MTA longitudinal study. *Journal of the American Academy of Child and Adolescent Psychiatry, 59,* 692-702.

Molina, B., & Pelham, W. (2014). Attention-Deficit/Hyperactivity Disorder and risk of substance abuse disorder: Developmental considerations, potential pathways, and opportunities for research. *Annual review of psychology, 10,* 607-639.

Molina, B., & Sibley, M. (2014). The case for including informant reports in the assessment of adulthood ADHD. *The ADHD Report, 22,* 1-6.

Momany, A., Kamradt, J., & Nikolas, M. (2017). A meta-analysis of the association between birth weight and attention deficit hyperactivity disorder. *Journal of Abnormal Child Psychology,* Advance on line publication, 11/21/17.

Murphy, K., & Appelbaum, K., (2017). How reliable are prevalence rates of ADHD in prisons? *The ADHD Report, 25,* 1-5.

Musser, E., & Nigg, J. (2017). Emotion dysregulation across emotion systems in Attention Deficit Hyperactivity Disorder. *Journal of Clinical Child and Adolescent Psychology,* Advance on line publication, 1/1/17.

Musser, E., Peris, T., Karalunas, S., Dieckman, N., & Nigg, J. (2016). Attention-Deficit/Hyperactivity Disorder developmental trajectories related to expressed parental emotion. *Journal of Abnormal Psychology, 125,* 182-195.

Narad, M., Kennelly, M., Zhang, N., Wade, S., Yeates, K., Taylor, H., Epstein, J., … Kurkowski, B. (2018). Secondary Attention-Deficit/Hyperactivity Disorder in children and adolescents 5 to 10 years after traumatic brain injury. *JAMA Pediatrics, 172,* 437-443.

Neta, M., Nelson, S., & Petersen, S. (2017). Dorsal anterior cingulate, medial superior frontal cortex, and anterior insula show performance reporting-related late task control signals. *Cerebral Cortex, March,* 2154-2165.

Neuhaus, E., & Beauhaine, T. (2017). Impulsivity and vulnerability to psychopathology. In T. Beauchaine & S. Hinshaw (Eds.), *Child and adolescent psychopathology* (3rd ed., pp. 178-212). Hoboken NJ: Wiley.

Nguyen, H., & Loughran, T. (2018). On the measurement and identification of turning points in criminology. *Annual review of criminology, 1,* 335-358.

NICE (2018). Attention-deficit hyperactivity disorder diagnosis and management. *NICE guideline, March 14,* 1-62.

Nigg, J. (2016). Attention and impulsivity. In D. Cicchetti (Ed.). *Developmental psychopathology: Risk, disorder and adaptation* (3rd ed., vol 3., 591-646). New York: Wiley.

—. (2017a). Attention-Deficit/Hyperactivity Disorder. In T. Beauchaine & S. Hinshaw (Eds.), *Child and adolescent psychopathology* (3rd ed., 407-448). New York: John Wiley & Sons.

—. (2017b). *Getting ahead of ADHD.* New York: Guilford Press.

—. (2017c). Annual research review: On the relations among self-regulation, self-control, executive functioning, effortful control, cognitive control, impulsivity, risk-taking, and inhibition for developmental psychopathology. *Journal of Child Psychology and Psychiatry, 58,* 361-383.

Nigg, J., Elmore, A., Natarajan, N., Friderici, K., & Nicholas, M. (2016). Variation in an iron metabolism gene moderates the association between blood lead levels and Attention-Deficit/Hyperactivity Disorder in children. *Psychological Science,27,* 257-269.

Nigg, J., & Song, M. (2018). ADHD and early experience: Revisiting the case for low birth weight. *Pediatrics, 141,* 1-2.

Nigg, J. (2018). Toward an emerging paradigm for understanding Attention-Deficit/Hyperactivity Disorder and other neurodevelopmental mental and behavioral disorders: Environmental risks and epigenetic mechanisms. *JAMA Pediatrics,* Advance on line publication.

Nock, M., Kazdin, A., Hiripi, E., & Kessler, R. (2007). Lifetime prevalence, correlates, and persistence of oppositional defiant disorder: results from the National Comorbidity survey replication. *Journal of Child Psychology, 48,* 703-713.

Noordermeer, S., Luman, M., Weeda, W., Buitelaar, J., Richards, J., Hartman, C., Hoekstra, P., …Ossterlaan, J. (2017). Risk factors of oppositional defiant disorder in attention deficit hyperactivity disorder. *European Child and Adolescent Psychiatry, 26,* 1155-1164.

Nordsletten, A., Larsson, H., Crowley, J., Almqvist, C., Lichtenstein, P., & Mataix-Cols, D. (2016). Patterns of nonrandom mating within and across 11 major psychiatric disorders. *JAMA Psychiatry, 73,* 354-361.

Ostergaard, S., Dalsgaard, S., Faraone, S., Munk-Olsen, T., & Laursen, T. (2017). Teen-age parenthood and birth rates for individuals with and without attention-deficit/hyperactivity disorder: A nationwide cohort study. *Journal of the American Academy of Child and Adolescent Psychiatry, 56,* 578-584.

Owens E, Cardoos S, Hinshaw S. (2015). Developmental progression and gender differences in individuals with ADHD. In Barkley, R. (4th ed), *Attention-Deficit/Hyperactivity Disorder: A handbook for diagnosis and treatment* (4th ed., pp, 223-255). New York: Guilford Press.

Quinn, P., Chang, Z., Hur, K., Gibbons, R., Lahey, B., Rickett, M., Sjolander, A., … D'Onofrio, B. (2017). ADHD medication and substance-related problems. *American Journal of Psychiatry, 174,* 877-885.

Page, T. (2007). Parallel play. *The New Yorker, August 7,* 1-6.

Park, J., Hudec, K., & Johnston, C. (2017). Parental ADHD symptoms and parenting behaviors: A meta-analysis. *Clinical Psychology Review, 56,* 25-39.

Pelham, W., & Fabiano, G. (2008). Evidence based psychosocial treatments for attention deficit/hyperactivity disorder. *Journal of Clinical Child and Adolescent Psychology, 37*, 184-214.

Petrovic, P., & Castellanos, F. (2016). Top-down dysregulation: From ADHD to emotional instability. *Frontiers in Behavioral Neuroscienc, 10,* 1-25.

Pingault, J., Cote, S., Lacourse, E., Galera, C., Vitaro, F., & Tremblay, R. (2016). Childhood hyperactivity, physical aggression and criminality: A 19-year prospective population-based study. *PLOS ONE, 8,* e2594.

Piquero, A., Gonzalez, J., & Jennings, W. (2015). Developmental trajectories and antisocial behavior over the life-course. In J. Morizot and L. Kazemian (Eds.), *The development of criminal and antisocial behavior* (pp. 75-88). Switzerland: Springer International Publishing.

Polanczyk, G., Willcutt, E., Salum, G., Kieling, C. & Rohde, L. (2014). ADHD prevalence estimates across three decades: an updated systematic review and meta-regression analysis. *International Journal of Epidemiology, 43,* 434-442.

Polis, B. (2003). *Only a mother could love him.* ADDHelpGuide.

Posner, M., Park, C., & Wang, Z. (2014). Connecting the dots: A review of resting state connectivity MRI studies in attention-deficit/ hyperactivity disorder. *Neuropsychology Review, 24,* 3-15.

Posner, M., Rothbart, M., & Voelker, P. (2016). Developing brain networks of attention. *Current Opinion in Pediatrics, 28,* 720-724.

Poulton, R., Moffitt, T., & Silva, P. (2015). The Dunnedin Multidisciplinary health and development study: overview of the first 40 years, with an eye to the future. *Social Psychiatry and Psychiatric Epidemiology, 50,* 679-673.

Prince, J., Wilens, T., Spencer, T., & Biederman, J. (2015). Pharmacotherapy of ADHD in adults. . In R. Barkley (Ed.), *Attention-deficit hyperactivity disorder*, (4th ed., pp. 826-860). New York: Guilford Press.

Rabinovitz, B., Rajendran, K., O'Neill, S., & Halperin, J. (2016). Temperament, executive control, and Attention-deficit/Hyperactivity Disorder across early development. *Journal of Abnormal Psychology, 125,* 196-206.

Raine, A. (2018). Antisocial personality as a neurodevelopmental disorder. *Annual Review of Clinical Psychology, 14,* 259-289.

Ramsay, J. (2015). Psychological assessment of adults with ADHD. In R. Barkley (Ed.), *Attention-deficit hyperactivity disorder*, (4th ed., pp. 475-500). New York: Guilford Press.

Raznahan, A., Shaw, P., LaLonde, F., Stockman, M., Wallace, G., Dede, G., … Giedd, J. (2011). How does your cortex grow? *The Journal of Neuroscience, 31,* 7174-7177.

Roberts, B., Martel, M., & Nigg, J. (2017). Are there executive dysfunction subtypes within ADHD? *Journal of Attention Disorders, 21,* 284-293.

Roberts, W., Milich, R., & Barkley, R. (2015). Primary symptoms, diagnostic criteria, subtyping, and prevalence of ADHD. In R. Barkley (Ed.), *Attention-deficit hyperactivity disorder*, (4th ed., pp. 50-80). New York: Guilford Press.

Robins, L. (1966). *Deviant children grown up: A sociological and psychiatric study of sociopathic personality*. Huntington New York: Robert E. Krieger Publishing Company.

—. (1978). Sturdy childhood predictors of adult antisocial behavior: Replications from longitudinal studies. *Psychological Medicine, 8,* 611- 622.

Rodenacker, K., Hautmann, C., Gortz-Dorlen, A., & Dopfner, M. (2018). Evidence for the trait-impulsivity etiological model in a clinical sample: Bifactor structure and its relationship to impairment and environmental risk. *Journal of Abnormal Child Psychology 46,* 659-669.

Rooney, M., & Pfiffner, L. (2018). Attention-deficit/Hyperactivity Disorder. In J. Butcher & P. Kendal (Eds.), *APA handbook of psychopathology: Child and adolescent psychopathology* (417-445). Washington DC: American Psychological Association.

Ros, R., & Graziano, P. (2018). Social functioning in children with or at risk for attention-deficit/hyperactivity disorder: A meta-analytic review *Journal of Clinical Child and Adolescent Psychology, 47,* 213-235.

Roy, A., & Hechtman, L. (2017). The multimodal treatment study of children with ADHD follow-up study: Outcomes and their predictors. In L. Hechtman (Ed.), *Attention-Deficit/Hyperactivity Disorder: Adult outcome and its predictors* (231-260). New York: Oxford University Press.

Rubia, K. (2018). Cognitive neuroscience of attention-deficit hyperactivity disorder (ADHD) and its clinical translation. *Frontiers in Human Neuroscience, 12* (March), 1-20.

Rubia, K., Alegria, A., Cubilo, A., Smith, A., Brammer, M., & Radua, J. (2014). Effects of stimulants on brain function in Attention-Deficit/Hyperactivity Disorder: A systematic review and meta-analysis. *Biological Psychiatry, 76*, 616-628.

Rutter, M. (2016). Research review: Child psychiatric diagnosis and classification: concepts, findings, challenges and potential. *Journal of Child Psychology and Psychiatry, 52*, 647-660.

Rutter, M., & Thapar, A. (2016). Using natural experiments to test environmental mediation hypotheses. In D. Cicchetti (Ed.), *Developmental psychopathology: Theory and method* (3rd ed., pp.,129-155.).

Saez, B., Serva, M., Becker, S., & Burns, G. (2018). Optimal items for assessing sluggish cognitive tempo in children across mother, father, and teacher ratings. *Journal of Clinical Child and Adolescent Psychology,* Advance on line publication, 2/16/18.

Safer, D. (2018). Is ADHD really increasing in youth? *Journal of Attention Disorders, 22,* 107-115.

Satteıfield, J, Faller, K., Crinella, F. Scheli, A., Swanson, J., & Homer, L. (2007). A 30-year prospective follow-up study of hyperactive boys with conduct problems: A adult criminology. *Journal of the American Academy of Child and Adolescent Psychiatry, 46,* 601-610.

Savage, J., Ferguson, C., & Flores, L. (2017). The effect of academic achievement on aggression and violent behavior: A meta-analysis. *Aggression and Violent Behavior, 37,* 91-101.

Sayal, K., Prasad, P., Daley, D., Ford, T., & Coghill, D. (2018). ADHD in children and young people: prevalence care pathways, and service provision. *The Lancet Psychiatry, 5,* 175-186.

Schechter, J., & Kollins, S. (2017). Prenatal smoke exposure and ADHD: Advancing the field. *Pediatrics, 139,* 1-2.

Sciberras, E., Mulraney, M., Silva, D., & Coghill, D. (2017). Prenatal risk factors and the etiology of ADHD—Review of existing evidence. *Current Psychiatry Reports, 19,*

Sharma, L., Markon, K., & Clarke, L. (2014). Toward a theory of distinct types of "impulsive" behaviors: A meta-analysis of self-report and behavioral measures. *Psychological Bulletin, 140,* 374-408.

Shaw, D. (2013). Future directions for research on the development and prevention of early conduct problems. *Journal of Clinical Child and Adolescent Psychology, 42, 18-428.*

Shaw, P., Ahn, K., & Rapoport, J. (2017). Good news for screening adult attention-deficit/hyperactivity disorder. *JAMA Psychiatry, 74,* 527.

Shaw, P., Stringaris, A., Nigg, J., & Leibenluft, E. (2014). Emotional dysregulation and attention-deficit/hyperactivity disorder. *American Journal of Psychiatry, 171,* 276-293.

Sibley, M., Coxe, S., & Molina, B. (2017). Refining diagnostic procedures for adults with ADHD. *Assessment, 24,* 290-296.

Sibley, M., & Kuriyan, A. (2016). DSM-5 changes enhance parent identification of symptoms in adolescents with ADHD. *Psychiatry Research, 242,* 180-185.

Sibley, M., Rohde, L., Swanson, J., Hechtman, L., Molina, B., Mitchell, J. …Stehl, M. (2018) Late-onset ADHD re-considered with comprehensive repeated assessments between ages 10 and 25. *American Journal of Psychiatry, 172,* 140-149.

Sibley, M., Swanson, J., Arnold, L., Hechtman, L., Owens, E., Stehli, A. …Pelham, W. (2017). Defining ADHD symptom persistence in adulthood: optimizing sensitivity and specificity. *Journal of Child Psychology and Psychiatry, 58,* 655-662.

Silverstein, M., Faraone, S., Alperin, S., Leon, T., Biederman, J., Spencer, T., Adler, A. (2018). Validation of the expanded versions of the Adult Self-Report Scale v1.1 symptom checklist and Adult ADHD Investigation Symptom Rating Scale. *Assessment,* Advance on line publication, 2/8/18

Smith, B., & Shapiro, C. (2015). Combined treatments for ADHD. In R. Barkley (Ed.), *Attention-deficit hyperactivity disorder*, (4th ed., pp. 686-704). New York: Guilford Press.

Snyder, J. (2016). Coercive family processes in the development of externalizing behavior: incorporating neurobiology into intervention research. In T. Beauchaine & S. Hinshaw (Eds.), *The Oxford handbook of spectrum disorders* (286-302). New York: Oxford University Press.

Solanto, M. (2018). The prevalence of "late-onset" ADHD in a clinically referred adult sample. *Journal of Attention Disorders,* Advance on line publication, 4/9/18.

Spencer, T., Brown, A., Seidman, L., Valera, E., Makris, N., Lomedico, A., Faraone, S., …Biederaman, J. ()2013). Effect of psychostimulants on brain structure and function in ADHD. A qualitative literature review of MRI-based neuroimaging studies. *Journal of Clinical Psychiatry, 74,* 902-917.

Spencer, A., Faraone, S., Bogucki, O., Pope, M. Uchida, M., Milad, M., Spencer, T. , … K. Biederman, J. (2016).Examining the Association Between Posttraumatic Stress Disorder and Attention-Deficit/Hyperactivity Disorder: A Systematic Review and Meta-Analysis. *Journal of Clinical Psychiatry, 77,* 72-83.

State, M., & Thapar, A. (2015). Genetics. In A. Thapar, D. Pine, J. Leckman, S. Scott, M. Snowling, & E. Taylor (Eds.), *Rutter's child and adolescent psychiatry* (6th ed., pp., 303-316). New York: Wiley.

Stevens, S., Sonuga-Barke, E., Kreppner, J., Beckett, C., Castle, J., Colvert, E., Groothues,. … Ruttter, M. (2008). Inattention/overactivity following early severe institutional deprivation: presentation and associations in early adolescence. *Journal of Abnormal Child Psychology, 36,* 385-398.

Stevens, J., & Wilens, T. (2015). Stimulant medication in children and adolescents. In L. Adler, T. Spencer, & T. Wilens, (Eds.). *Attention-Deficit Hyperactivity Disorder in children and adults* (245-258). Cambridge: Cambridge University Press.

Storebo, O., Krough, H., Ramstad, E., Moreira-Maia, C., Holmskov, M., Skoog, M., Nilaausen, T., …Gluud, C. (2015). Methylphenidate in attention-deficit/ hyperactivity disorder in children and adolescents: Cochrane systematic reviews with meta-analyses and trial sequential analyses of randomized clinical trials. *BMJ, 351,* h5203.

Stringaris, A., & Goodman, R. (2009). Longitudinal outcome of youth oppositionality: irritable, headstrong, and hurtful behaviors. *Journal of the American Academy of Child and Adolescent Psychiatry, 48,* 404-412.

Swanson, J., Wigal, T., Jensen, P., Mitchell, J., Weisner, T. , Murray, D., Arnold, L., …Stehli, A. (2018). The qualitative interview study of persistent and nonpersistent substance use in the MTA: Sample, characteristics, frequent use, and reasons for use. *Journal of Attention Disorders, 22,* 21-37.

Thapar, A., & Cooper, M. (2016). Attention-deficit/hyperactivity disorder. *Lancet, 387,* 1240-1250.

Thapar, A., Cooper, M., & Rutter, M. (2017). Neurodevelopmental disorders. *Lancet Psychiatry, 4,* 339-346.

Thomas, R., Sanders, S., Doust, J., Beller, E., & Glasziou, P. (2015). Prevalence of Attention-deficit hyperactivity disorder: A systematic review of meta-analysis. *Pediatrics, 135, e*994-e1001.

Tramontana, M., Cowan, R., Zald, D., Prokop, J., & Guillamondegui, O. (2014). Traumatic brain injury-related deficits: Treatment outcomes and lisdexamfetamine dimesylate (Vyvanse). *Brain Injury, 28,* 1461-1472.

Tremblay, R., Vitaro, F., & Cote, S. (2018). Developmental origins of chronic physical aggression: A bio-psycho-social model for the next generation of prevention interventions. *Annual review of psychology, 68,* 383-407.

Trestman, R., Champion, M., Ford, E., Metzner, J., Newkirk, C., Penn, J., Penn, J., …Young, J. (2016). *Psychiatric services in correctional facilities* (3rd ed.): Arlington, VA: American Psychiatric Association.

Tryon, W. (2016). Replication is about effect size: Comment on Maxwell, Lau, and Howard (2015). *American Psychologist, 71,* 236-237.

Uchida, M., & Biederman, J. (2017). Young adult outcome of attention-deficit/hyperactivity disorder. In. L. Hechtman (Ed.), *Attention Deficit Hyperactivity Disorder: Adult outcome and its predictors* (157-178.). New York: Oxford University Press.

Uddin, L., & Karlsgodt, K., (2018). Future directions for examination of brain networks in neurodevelopmental disorders. *Journal of Clinical Child and Adolescent Psychology, 47,* 1-15.

Ustan, B., Adler, L., Rudin, C., Faraone, S., Spencer, T., Berglund, P. … Kessler, R. (2017). The World Health Organization adult attention-deficit/hyperactivity disorder self-report screening scale for DSM-5. *JAMA Psychiatry, 74,* 52-526.

Van der Mass, M., Kolla, N., Erickson, P., Wickens, C., Mann, R., & Vingilis, E. (2018). Examining the effect of social bonds on the relationship between ADHD and past arrest in a representative sample of adults. *Criminal Behaviour and Mental Health, 28,* 120-131.

Vande Voort, J., He, J., Jameson, N., & Merikangas, K. (2014). Impact of the DSM-5 of Attention-deficit Hyperactivity Disorder: Age-of-onset criterion in the US adolescent population. *Journal of the American Academy of Child and Adolescent Psychiatry, 53,* 736-744.

Van Emmerick-van Oortmerssen, K., Glind, G., van den Brink, W., Smit, F., Crunele, C., Swets, M., & Schoevers, R. (2012). Prevalence of attention-deficit hyperactivity disorder in substance use disorder patients: a meta-analysis and meta-regression analysis. *Drug and Alcohol Dependence*, *122*, 11-19.

Van IJzendoorn, M., Palacios, M., Sonuga-Barke, E., Gunnar, M., Vorria, P., McCall, R., … & Juffer, F. (2011). Children in institutional care: Delayed development and resilience. *Monographs for the Society in Child Development, 76,* 8-30.

Vazsonyi, A., Mikuska, J., & Kelley, E. (2017). Its time: A meta-analysis on the self-control deviance link. *Journal of Criminal Justice, 48,* 48-53.

Venter, C. (2007). *A life decoded.* New York: Viking Press.

Visser, S., Danielson, M., Bitsko, R., Holbrook, J., Kagan, M., Ghandour, R., Perou, R. …Blumburg, S. (2014). Trends in the parent-report of health care provider-diagnosed and medicated Attention-deficit Hyperactivity Disorder: United States, 2003-2011). *Journal of the American Academy of Child and Adolescent Psychiatry, 53,* 34-46.

Volkow, N., Koob, G., & McClellan, A. (2016). Neurobiologic advances from the brain disease model of addiction. *New England Journal of Medicine, 374,* 363-371.

Volkow, N., Wise, R., & Bayler, R. (2017). The dopamine motive system: implications for drug and food addiction. *Nature Review: Neuroscience, 18,* 741-751.

Wen, H., Hockenberry, J. & Cummings, J. (2014). The effect of substance use disorder treatment use on crime: Evidence from public insurance expansion and health insurance parity mandates. *National Bureau of Economic Research, October,* 1-38.

Wertz, J., Agnew-Blais, J., Caspi, A., Danese, A., Fisher, H., Goldman-Meollor, S., Moffitt, T., & Arseneault, L. (2018b). From childhood conduct problems to poor functioning at age 18 years: Examining explanations in a longitudinal cohort study. *Journal of the American Academy of Child and Adolescent Psychiatry, 57,* 54-60.

Wertz, J., Caspi, A., Belsky, J., Beckley, A., Arseneault, I., Barnes, J., Corcoran, D., …Moffitt, T. (2018a). Genetics and crime: Integrating new genetic discoveries into psychological research about behavior. *Psychological Science, 29,* 791-803.

Weyandt, L. & Gudmundsdottir, G. (2015). Developmental and neuropsychological deficits in children with ADHD. In R. Barkley (Ed.), *Attention-deficit hyperactivity disorder*, (4th ed., pp. 116-139). New York: Guilford Press.

White, H. (2016). Substance and crime. In K. Sher (Ed.), *The Oxford handbook of substance use and substance use disorder, Vol. 2* (pp. 347-377). New York: Oxford University Press.

White, H., Conway, F., Buckman, J., & Loeber, R. (2018). Does substance use exacerbate escalation along developmental pathways of covert and over externalizing behaviors among young men? *Journal of Developmental and Life Course Criminology, 4,* 137-147.

Widom, C. (2017). Long-term impact of childhood abuse and neglect on crime and violence. *Clinical Psychology Science and Practice, 24*, 186-202.

Wiggs, K., Chang, Z., Quinn, P., Hur, K., Gibbons, R., Dunn, D., Birkell, I., … D'Onofrio, B. (2018). Attention-deficit/hyperactivity disorder medication and seizures. *Neurology, 90,* 1104-1110.

Wilens, T., & Morrison, N. (2015). Attention-deficit/Hyperactivity Disorder and the substance use disorders in ADHD. In L. Adler, T. Spencer, & T. Wilens (Eds.), *Attention-Deficit/Hyperactivity Disorder in adults and children* (pp. 111-122). New York: Cambridge University Press.

Willcutt, E. (2012). The prevalence of DSM-IV Attention-deficit Hyperactivity Disorder: A meta-analytic review. *Neurotherapeutics, 9,* 490-499.

—. (2015). Theories of ADHD. In R. Barkley (Ed.), *Attention-deficit hyperactivity disorder*, (4th ed., pp. 391-404). New York: Guilford Press.

Wolpert, M., & Ford, T. (2015). Using epidemiology to plan organize, and evaluate services for children and adolescents with mental health problems. In A. Thapar, D., Pine, J. Leckman, S. Scott, M. Snowling, & E. Taylor (Eds.), *Rutter's child and adolescent psychiatry,* (6th ed., 163-176). New York: Wiley.

Yeates, K. Traumatic brain injury. In *Pediatric Neuropsychology: Theory, Research and Practice* (2nd ed.). K.Yeates, M. Ris, H. Taylor, B. Pennington (Eds), Guilford Press, New York, 112-146 (2010).

Yoncheva, Y. Samandepali, K., Reiss, P., Kelly, C., Martino, A., Lazar, M., … Castellanos, F. (2016). Mode of anisotropy reveals global diffusion alternations in Attention-Deficit/Hyperactivity Disorder. *Journal of the American Academy of Child and Adolescent Psychiatry, 55,* 137-145.

Young, S. (2014). ADHD in prisons: treat the offenders and reduce crime. *EBC News, Autumn,* 18.

—. (2015). *Child evaluation: A diagnostic interview of ADHD in children.* London: Psychology Services Limited.

—. (2017). A disappointing review of prevalence rates of ADHD in prisons. *Blog Post, April 16.*

Young, S., Adamou, M., Bolea, B., Gufjonsson, G., Muller, U., Pitts, M., … Asherson, P. (2011). The identification and management of ADHD offenders within the criminal justice system: a consensus statement from the UK adult ADHD network and criminal justice agencies. *BMC Psychiatry, 11,* 1-14.

Young, S., Gonzalez, R., Mullens, H., Mutch, L., Malet-Lambert, I., & Gudjonsson, G. (2018). Neurodevelopmental disorders in prison inmates: comorbidity and combined associations with psychiatric symptoms and behavioural disturbance. *Psychiatric Research, 261,* 109-115.

Young S., González R., Mutch L., Mallet-Lambert I., O'Rourke L., Hickey N., Asherson P., & Gudjonsson G.(2016). Diagnostic accuracy of a brief screening tool for Attention Deficit/Hyperactivity Disorder in UK prison inmates. *Psychological Medicine*, *46*, 1449-1458.

Young, S., Moss, D., Sedgwick, O., Fridman, M., & Hodgkins, P. (2015) A meta-analysis of the prevalence of attention-deficit/hyperactivity disorder in incarcerated populations. *Psychological Medicine, 45,* 247-258.

Zastrow, B., Martel, M., & Widiger, T. (2016). Preschool oppositional defiant disorder: a disorder of negative affect, surgency, and disagreeableness. *Journal of Clinical Child and Adolescent Psychology, 1/21/16.*

Zisner, A., & Beauchaine, T. (2016a). Midbrain neural mechanisms of trait impulsivity. In T. Beauchaine & S. Hinshaw (Eds.), *The Oxford handbook of externalizing spectrum disorders* (184-200). New York: Oxford University Press.

Zisner, A., & Beauchaine, T. (2016b). Neural substrates of trait impulsivity, anhedonia, and irritability: Mechanisms of heterotypic comorbidity between externalizing disorders and unipolar depression. *Development and Psychopathology, 28,* 1179-1210.

Zuckerman, M. (2007). *Sensation seeking and risky behavior.* Washington DC: American Psychological Association Press.

Zuk, O., Hechter, E., Sunyaev, S., & Lander, E. (2012). The mystery of missing heritability: Genetic interactions create phantom heritability. *PNAS, 109,* 1193-1198.

APPENDIX 1

Methylphenidate-based Stimulants

Delivery	Brand Name	Duration	Form	Available Dosage Strengths	Concerns & Side Effects
Immediate release	**Focalin®** *(generic available)*	4–6 hours	tablet	2.5 mg 5 mg 10 mg	Common side effects include: ☐ headache ☐ decreased appetite ☐ stomach ache ☐ nervousness ☐ trouble sleeping ☐ nausea Other serious side effects include: ☐ slowing of growth (height and weight) in children ☐ seizures, mainly in patients with a history of seizures ☐ eyesight changes or blurred vision ☐ painful and prolonged erections
	Methylin® Oral Solution *(generic available)*	3–4 hours	liquid	5 mg/5ml 10 mg/5ml	
	Ritalin® *(generic available)*	3–4 hours	tablet	5 mg 10 mg 20 mg	
Sustained release	**Ritalin-SR®** *(generic available)*	4–8 hours	tablet	20 mg	

	Desoxyn® *(generic available)*	4-8 hours	tablet	5 mg	Heart-related problems: □ sudden death in patients who have heart problems or heart defects □ stroke and heart attack in adults □ increased blood pressure and heart rate Mental (Psychiatric) Problems: All Patients • new or worse behavior and thought problems • new or worse bipolar illness • new or worse aggressive behavior or hostility Children and Teenagers • new psychotic symptoms (such as hearing voices, believing things that are not true, are suspicious) or new manic symptoms Circulation problems in fingers and toes
Extended release	**Aptensio XR™**	12 hours	capsule	10 mg 15 mg 20 mg 30 mg 40 mg 50 mg 60 mg	
	Concerta®* *(generic available)*	10–12 hours	tablet	18 mg 27 mg 36 mg 54 mg	
	Cotempla™XR-ODT	12 hours	tablet	8.6 mg 17.3 mg 25.9 mg	
	Daytrana®	10–12 hours (9 hours applied + up to three hours after)	transdermal patch	10 mg 15 mg 20mg 30mg	
	Focalin XR® *(generic available)*	6–10 hours	capsule	5 mg 10 mg 15 mg 20 mg 30 mg 40 mg	
	Metadate CD®	8–10 hours	capsule	10 mg 20 mg	

	(generic available)			30 mg	
	Ritalin LA® *(generic available)*	8–10 hours	capsule	10 mg 20 mg 30 mg 40 mg	
	QuilliChew ER™	8 hours	chewable tablet	20 mg 30 mg 40 mg	
	Quillivant XR®	8, 10, and 12 hours	liquid	10 mg 20 mg	

*The FDA issued a report that two generic versions of Concerta delivered the active medication at a slower rate and might not work as well as the brand version.

Amphetamine-based Stimulants

Delivery	Brand Name	Duration	Form	Available Dosage Strengths	Concerns & Side Effects
Immediate release	**Adderall ®** *(generic available)*	4–6 hours	tablet	5 mg 7.5 mg 10 mg 12.5 mg 15 mg 20 mg 30 mg	Common side effects include: • headache • trouble sleeping • circulation problems in fingers and toes • decreased appetite • nervousness

	Evekeo®	4–6 hours	capsule	5 mg 10 mg	• dizziness • diarrhea, constipation • mood changes, feeling irritable, restless or nervous • dry mouth, unusual or unpleasant taste in mouth • runny nose, nosebleeds • itching, rash, or allergic reactions • increased tics • impotence or sexual problems Other serious side effects include: • slowing of growth (height and weight) in children • seizures, mainly in patients with a history of seizures • eyesight changes or blurred vision Heart-related problems: • sudden death in patients who have heart problems or heart defects • stroke and heart attack in adults
	ProCentra®	4-6 hours	liquid	5mg/5ml	
	Zenzedi®	4–5 hours	tablet	2.5 mg 5 mg 7.5 mg 10 mg 15 mg 20 mg 30 mg	
Extended release	**Adderall XR®** *(generic available)*	8–12 hours	capsule	5 mg 10 mg 15 mg 20 mg 25 mg 30 mg	
	Adzenys XR-ODT™	9–10 hours—children 11 hours—adults	tablet	3.1 mg 6.3 mg 9.4 mg 12.5 mg 15.7 mg 18.8 mg	
	Dexedrine® *(generic available)*	8–10 hours	capsule	5 mg 10 mg 15 mg	
	Dyanavel® XR	13 hours	liquid	2.5 mg 5 mg 7.5 mg 10 mg	

				12.5 mg 15 mg 17.5 mg 20 mg	• increased blood pressure and heart rate Mental (Psychiatric) problems: All Patients • new or worse behavior and thought problems • new or worse bipolar illness • new or worse aggressive behavior or hostility Children and Teenagers • new psychotic symptoms (such as hearing voices, believing things that are not true, are suspicious) or new manic symptoms High potential for misuse and abuse: Administration for prolonged periods of time may lead to drug dependence May impair ability to drive or operate heavy machinery
	Mydayis™	16 hours	capsule	12.5 mg 25 mg 37.5 mg 50 mg	
	Vyvanse®	10–12 hours	capsule	20 mg 50 mg 30 mg 60 mg 40 mg 70 mg	

Nonstimulant Medications

Medication	Brand Name	Delivery	Duration	Form	Available Dosage Strengths	Concerns & Side Effects
Atomoxetine	**Strattera®** *(generic available)*	Extended release	24 hours	capsule	10 mg 18mg 25 mg 40mg 60 mg 80mg 100 mg	Nervousness, sleep problems, fatigue, upset stomach, dizziness, dry mouth. In rare cases, may lead to severe liver injury or possibly to suicidal thoughts.

Antihypertensives

Medication	Brand Name	Delivery	Duration	Form	Available Dosage Strengths	Concerns & Side Effects
Clonidine	**Kapvay®** *(generic available)*	Extended release	12–24 hours	tablet	0.1 mg 0.2 mg	Fatigue, drowsiness, dizziness, dry mouth, decreased appetite, constipation, irritability, low blood pressure; abrupt discontinuation may lead to elevated levels of nervousness, anxiety, and blood pressure
Guanfacine	**Intuniv®** *(generic available)*	Extended release	12–24 hours	tablets	1 mg 2 mg 3 mg 4 mg	

This chart is supported by Cooperative Agreement Number NU38DD005376 from the Centers for Disease Control and Prevention (CDC). The contents are solely the responsibility of the authors and do not necessarily represent the official views of CDC.